50 Nutrient-Packed Recipes for Home

By: Kelly Johnson

Table of Contents

- Grilled Salmon with Lemon-Dill Sauce
- Quinoa and Black Bean Stuffed Peppers
- Kale and Chickpea Salad with Lemon-Tahini Dressing
- Sweet Potato and Chickpea Curry
- Spinach and Feta Stuffed Chicken Breast
- Lentil and Vegetable Soup
- Avocado and Tomato Salsa
- Baked Cod with Garlic and Herb Crust
- Cucumber and Avocado Salad
- Turkey and Vegetable Stir-Fry
- Roasted Brussels Sprouts with Balsamic Glaze
- Chickpea and Spinach Coconut Curry
- Zucchini Noodles with Pesto and Cherry Tomatoes
- Grilled Chicken with Mango Salsa
- Quinoa Salad with Roasted Vegetables
- Baked Eggplant Parmesan
- Shrimp and Broccoli Stir-Fry
- Greek Salad with Feta and Olives
- Teriyaki Tofu Lettuce Wraps
- Cauliflower Fried Rice
- Black Bean and Corn Salsa
- Lemon Garlic Roasted Shrimp
- Stuffed Portobello Mushrooms with Quinoa and Spinach
- Turkey and Sweet Potato Chili
- Caprese Salad with Balsamic Glaze
- Pesto Zoodles with Cherry Tomatoes
- Salmon and Asparagus Foil Packets
- Mediterranean Chickpea Quinoa Bowl
- Broccoli and Cheddar Stuffed Chicken Breast
- Butternut Squash and Lentil Soup
- Chicken and Vegetable Skewers
- Brussels Sprouts and Bacon Hash
- Quinoa and Kale Patties
- Baked Cod with Tomato and Olive Tapenade
- Roasted Red Pepper and Chickpea Wrap

- Turkey and Spinach Meatballs
- Sweet Potato and Black Bean Quesadillas
- Grilled Vegetable Platter with Hummus
- Shrimp and Avocado Salad
- Spaghetti Squash with Tomato and Basil Sauce
- Lentil and Kale Stuffed Bell Peppers
- Chicken and Quinoa Lettuce Wraps
- Roasted Beet and Goat Cheese Salad
- Miso-Glazed Eggplant
- Cabbage and Apple Slaw
- Baked Teriyaki Salmon
- Broccoli and Cauliflower Gratin
- Quinoa and Black Bean Burgers
- Grilled Turkey and Veggie Kabobs
- Zesty Cilantro Lime Cauliflower Rice

Grilled Salmon with Lemon-Dill Sauce

Ingredients:

For the Grilled Salmon:

- 4 salmon fillets
- 2 tablespoons olive oil
- Salt and black pepper to taste
- Lemon wedges for serving

For the Lemon-Dill Sauce:

- 1/2 cup Greek yogurt
- 2 tablespoons fresh dill, chopped
- 1 tablespoon lemon juice
- 1 teaspoon lemon zest
- 1 clove garlic, minced
- Salt and black pepper to taste

Instructions:

Grilled Salmon:

> Preheat the Grill:
> - Preheat your grill to medium-high heat.
>
> Prepare the Salmon:
> - Pat the salmon fillets dry with paper towels. Brush both sides with olive oil and season with salt and black pepper.
>
> Grill the Salmon:
> - Place the salmon fillets on the preheated grill, skin side down. Grill for about 4-5 minutes per side, or until the salmon is cooked through and easily flakes with a fork.
>
> Serve:
> - Transfer the grilled salmon to a serving platter. Squeeze fresh lemon wedges over the fillets.

Lemon-Dill Sauce:

> Prepare the Sauce:
> - In a small bowl, mix together Greek yogurt, chopped fresh dill, lemon juice, lemon zest, minced garlic, salt, and black pepper.
>
> Serve:

- Spoon the lemon-dill sauce over the grilled salmon fillets or serve it on the side as a dipping sauce.

Garnish (Optional):
- Garnish with additional fresh dill or lemon slices if desired.

This Grilled Salmon with Lemon-Dill Sauce is a delightful combination of flavors. The smokiness from the grill complements the richness of the salmon, while the lemon-dill sauce adds a zesty and herby kick. It's a perfect dish for a healthy and flavorful meal!

Quinoa and Black Bean Stuffed Peppers

Ingredients:

- 4 large bell peppers, halved and seeds removed
- 1 cup quinoa, rinsed
- 2 cups vegetable broth or water
- 1 can (15 oz) black beans, drained and rinsed
- 1 cup corn kernels (fresh or frozen)
- 1 cup diced tomatoes
- 1 cup shredded cheddar or Mexican blend cheese
- 1 teaspoon ground cumin
- 1 teaspoon chili powder
- 1/2 teaspoon garlic powder
- Salt and black pepper to taste
- Olive oil for drizzling
- Fresh cilantro or parsley for garnish (optional)
- Lime wedges for serving

Instructions:

Preheat the Oven:
- Preheat your oven to 375°F (190°C).

Prepare the Quinoa:
- In a medium saucepan, combine the quinoa and vegetable broth (or water). Bring to a boil, then reduce the heat to low, cover, and simmer for 15-20 minutes or until the quinoa is cooked and the liquid is absorbed.

Prepare the Peppers:
- While the quinoa is cooking, halve the bell peppers and remove the seeds and membranes. Place the pepper halves in a baking dish.

Mix the Filling:
- In a large bowl, combine the cooked quinoa, black beans, corn, diced tomatoes, shredded cheese, cumin, chili powder, garlic powder, salt, and black pepper. Mix well to combine.

Stuff the Peppers:
- Stuff each bell pepper half with the quinoa and black bean mixture, pressing down gently to pack the filling.

Drizzle with Olive Oil:
- Drizzle a little olive oil over the stuffed peppers.

Bake in the Oven:

- Bake in the preheated oven for 25-30 minutes or until the peppers are tender.

Garnish and Serve:
- Remove the stuffed peppers from the oven. Garnish with fresh cilantro or parsley if desired. Serve with lime wedges on the side.

These Quinoa and Black Bean Stuffed Peppers are a delicious and wholesome meal. They are packed with protein, fiber, and a variety of flavors. Enjoy them as a vegetarian main course or as a nutritious side dish!

Kale and Chickpea Salad with Lemon-Tahini Dressing

Ingredients:

For the Salad:

- 1 bunch kale, stems removed and leaves chopped
- 1 can (15 oz) chickpeas, drained and rinsed
- 1 cup cherry tomatoes, halved
- 1 cucumber, diced
- 1/4 cup red onion, finely chopped
- 1/4 cup feta cheese, crumbled
- 1/4 cup pumpkin seeds (pepitas)
- Salt and black pepper to taste

For the Lemon-Tahini Dressing:

- 1/4 cup tahini
- 3 tablespoons olive oil
- 2 tablespoons fresh lemon juice
- 1 tablespoon maple syrup or honey
- 1 clove garlic, minced
- 1/2 teaspoon ground cumin
- Salt and black pepper to taste
- Water (as needed to thin the dressing)

Instructions:

For the Salad:

   Massage the Kale:
   - Place the chopped kale in a large bowl. Drizzle with a bit of olive oil and a pinch of salt. Massage the kale with your hands for a few minutes to soften it.

   Assemble the Salad:
   - Add chickpeas, cherry tomatoes, cucumber, red onion, feta cheese, and pumpkin seeds to the bowl with kale.

   Toss:
   - Toss the salad ingredients together until well combined.

For the Lemon-Tahini Dressing:

Prepare the Dressing:
- In a small bowl, whisk together tahini, olive oil, fresh lemon juice, maple syrup (or honey), minced garlic, ground cumin, salt, and black pepper.

Adjust Consistency:
- If the dressing is too thick, add water a tablespoon at a time until you reach your desired consistency.

Taste and Adjust:
- Taste the dressing and adjust the seasonings according to your preference.

Serve:

Drizzle the Dressing:
- Drizzle the Lemon-Tahini Dressing over the salad.

Toss and Serve:
- Toss the salad until it's evenly coated with the dressing.

Garnish:
- Garnish with additional pumpkin seeds, feta cheese, or a sprinkle of black pepper if desired.

This Kale and Chickpea Salad with Lemon-Tahini Dressing is not only delicious but also packed with nutrients. It makes for a satisfying and wholesome meal on its own or can be served as a side dish. Enjoy the vibrant flavors and textures!

Sweet Potato and Chickpea Curry

Ingredients:

- 2 tablespoons coconut oil or olive oil
- 1 large onion, finely chopped
- 3 cloves garlic, minced
- 1 tablespoon fresh ginger, grated
- 2 large sweet potatoes, peeled and diced
- 1 can (15 oz) chickpeas, drained and rinsed
- 1 can (14 oz) diced tomatoes
- 1 can (14 oz) coconut milk
- 1 cup vegetable broth
- 2 tablespoons red curry paste
- 1 teaspoon ground turmeric
- 1 teaspoon ground cumin
- 1 teaspoon ground coriander
- 1 teaspoon paprika
- Salt and black pepper to taste
- Fresh cilantro, chopped (for garnish)
- Cooked rice or naan (for serving)

Instructions:

Saute Aromatics:
- In a large pot or deep skillet, heat the coconut oil over medium heat. Add chopped onions and sauté until they become translucent.

Add Garlic and Ginger:
- Add minced garlic and grated ginger to the pot. Cook for another 1-2 minutes until fragrant.

Add Spices:
- Stir in red curry paste, ground turmeric, ground cumin, ground coriander, paprika, salt, and black pepper. Cook for a minute to toast the spices.

Add Sweet Potatoes and Chickpeas:
- Add diced sweet potatoes and drained chickpeas to the pot. Mix well to coat them with the spice mixture.

Pour in Tomatoes, Coconut Milk, and Broth:
- Pour in diced tomatoes (with their juices), coconut milk, and vegetable broth. Stir to combine.

Simmer:

- Bring the curry to a simmer. Reduce the heat to low, cover, and let it simmer for about 20-25 minutes or until the sweet potatoes are tender.

Adjust Seasonings:
- Taste the curry and adjust the seasonings if needed. You can add more salt, pepper, or spices according to your preference.

Serve:
- Serve the Sweet Potato and Chickpea Curry over cooked rice or with naan bread.

Garnish:
- Garnish with chopped fresh cilantro before serving.

This Sweet Potato and Chickpea Curry is not only delicious but also packed with nutrients. It's a comforting and wholesome meal that can be enjoyed as a main course. Feel free to customize the spice levels and add your favorite vegetables if desired. Enjoy!

Spinach and Feta Stuffed Chicken Breast

Ingredients:

- 4 boneless, skinless chicken breasts
- Salt and black pepper to taste
- 2 cups fresh spinach, chopped
- 1/2 cup feta cheese, crumbled
- 1/4 cup sun-dried tomatoes, chopped
- 2 cloves garlic, minced
- 1 tablespoon olive oil
- 1 teaspoon dried oregano
- 1 teaspoon dried thyme
- 1 teaspoon paprika
- Toothpicks or kitchen twine (optional)
- Lemon wedges (for serving)

Instructions:

Preheat the Oven:
- Preheat your oven to 375°F (190°C).

Prepare the Chicken:
- Lay the chicken breasts flat on a cutting board. Use a sharp knife to cut a pocket into the side of each chicken breast, being careful not to cut all the way through. Season both sides of the chicken with salt and black pepper.

Make the Filling:
- In a skillet, heat olive oil over medium heat. Add minced garlic and cook for about 1 minute until fragrant. Add chopped spinach and cook until wilted. Remove from heat and stir in feta cheese, sun-dried tomatoes, dried oregano, dried thyme, and paprika. Mix until well combined.

Stuff the Chicken:
- Spoon the spinach and feta mixture into the pockets of each chicken breast, distributing it evenly. Secure the openings with toothpicks or use kitchen twine to tie the chicken breasts, ensuring the filling stays inside.

Sear the Chicken:
- In an oven-safe skillet, heat a bit of olive oil over medium-high heat. Sear the stuffed chicken breasts for 2-3 minutes per side until golden brown.

Bake in the Oven:

- Transfer the skillet to the preheated oven and bake for 20-25 minutes or until the chicken is cooked through (internal temperature of 165°F or 74°C).

Serve:
- Remove the toothpicks or twine before serving. Squeeze lemon wedges over the stuffed chicken breasts before serving.

Garnish (Optional):
- Garnish with additional fresh herbs or a sprinkle of feta cheese if desired.

Enjoy these Spinach and Feta Stuffed Chicken Breasts as a delightful and flavorful main course. They pair well with a side of roasted vegetables, rice, or a light salad.

Lentil and Vegetable Soup

Ingredients:

- 1 cup dry green or brown lentils, rinsed and drained
- 1 large onion, chopped
- 2 carrots, diced
- 2 celery stalks, diced
- 3 cloves garlic, minced
- 1 can (14 oz) diced tomatoes
- 6 cups vegetable broth
- 1 teaspoon ground cumin
- 1 teaspoon ground coriander
- 1/2 teaspoon smoked paprika
- 1/2 teaspoon dried thyme
- 1 bay leaf
- Salt and black pepper to taste
- 2 cups chopped kale or spinach
- 1 tablespoon olive oil
- Fresh lemon wedges (for serving)

Instructions:

Saute Vegetables:
- In a large pot, heat olive oil over medium heat. Add chopped onions, carrots, and celery. Saute for about 5 minutes until the vegetables are softened.

Add Garlic and Spices:
- Add minced garlic, ground cumin, ground coriander, smoked paprika, dried thyme, and bay leaf to the pot. Stir well and cook for an additional 1-2 minutes until the spices are fragrant.

Add Lentils and Broth:
- Add rinsed lentils, diced tomatoes (with their juices), and vegetable broth to the pot. Stir to combine.

Season and Simmer:
- Season the soup with salt and black pepper to taste. Bring the soup to a boil, then reduce the heat to low, cover, and simmer for about 25-30 minutes or until the lentils are tender.

Add Leafy Greens:

- Add chopped kale or spinach to the soup. Stir and cook for an additional 5 minutes until the greens are wilted.

Adjust Seasonings:
- Taste the soup and adjust the seasonings if needed. Remove the bay leaf.

Serve:
- Ladle the Lentil and Vegetable Soup into bowls. Squeeze fresh lemon juice over each serving before serving.

Garnish (Optional):
- Garnish with additional fresh herbs or a drizzle of olive oil if desired.

This Lentil and Vegetable Soup is a comforting and wholesome meal that's rich in protein and fiber. It's a great option for a satisfying lunch or dinner, especially during colder months. Enjoy!

Avocado and Tomato Salsa

Ingredients:

- 2 ripe avocados, diced
- 1 cup cherry tomatoes, halved or diced
- 1/4 cup red onion, finely chopped
- 1 jalapeño, seeds removed and finely chopped (optional, for heat)
- 1/4 cup fresh cilantro, chopped
- 1-2 cloves garlic, minced
- Juice of 1 lime
- Salt and black pepper to taste

Instructions:

Prepare the Ingredients:
- Dice the avocados, halve or dice the cherry tomatoes, finely chop the red onion, jalapeño, and cilantro, and mince the garlic.

Combine Ingredients:
- In a mixing bowl, combine the diced avocados, cherry tomatoes, red onion, jalapeño, cilantro, and minced garlic.

Add Lime Juice:
- Squeeze the juice of one lime over the ingredients. The lime not only adds flavor but also helps prevent the avocados from browning.

Season:
- Season the salsa with salt and black pepper to taste. Adjust the seasoning according to your preference.

Gently Toss:
- Gently toss the ingredients together until well combined. Be careful not to mash the avocados completely, leaving some chunks for texture.

Chill (Optional):
- If time allows, refrigerate the salsa for about 15-30 minutes to let the flavors meld.

Serve:
- Serve the Avocado and Tomato Salsa as a dip with tortilla chips, as a topping for tacos or grilled meats, or as a side dish for various meals.

Garnish (Optional):
- Garnish with additional cilantro or a slice of lime before serving.

This Avocado and Tomato Salsa is a vibrant and delicious addition to your meals. It's perfect for summer gatherings, picnics, or as a quick and healthy snack. Enjoy!

Baked Cod with Garlic and Herb Crust

Ingredients:

- 4 cod fillets (about 6 oz each)
- 2 tablespoons olive oil
- 2 cloves garlic, minced
- 1 tablespoon fresh parsley, chopped
- 1 teaspoon fresh thyme leaves (or 1/2 teaspoon dried thyme)
- 1 teaspoon fresh rosemary, chopped (or 1/2 teaspoon dried rosemary)
- 1 teaspoon lemon zest
- Salt and black pepper to taste
- Lemon wedges (for serving)

Instructions:

Preheat the Oven:
- Preheat your oven to 400°F (200°C).

Prepare the Cod Fillets:
- Pat the cod fillets dry with paper towels. Place them on a baking sheet lined with parchment paper.

Make the Herb Crust:
- In a small bowl, combine olive oil, minced garlic, chopped parsley, thyme, rosemary, lemon zest, salt, and black pepper. Mix well to create the herb crust.

Apply the Herb Crust:
- Brush the herb crust mixture over the top of each cod fillet, ensuring an even coating.

Bake in the Oven:
- Bake the cod fillets in the preheated oven for 12-15 minutes or until the fish is opaque and easily flakes with a fork.

Broil (Optional):
- If you prefer a golden crust, you can broil the cod for an additional 1-2 minutes, watching closely to prevent burning.

Serve:
- Carefully transfer the baked cod fillets to serving plates. Squeeze fresh lemon wedges over the top before serving.

Garnish (Optional):
- Garnish with additional chopped fresh herbs if desired.

This Baked Cod with Garlic and Herb Crust is a simple and elegant dish that's perfect for a quick weeknight dinner or a special occasion. Pair it with your favorite side dishes, such as roasted vegetables, rice, or a fresh salad, for a complete and delicious meal. Enjoy!

Cucumber and Avocado Salad

Ingredients:

- 2 cucumbers, thinly sliced
- 2 ripe avocados, diced
- 1/4 cup red onion, thinly sliced
- 1/4 cup fresh cilantro, chopped
- 1 tablespoon fresh dill, chopped
- 2 tablespoons extra-virgin olive oil
- 1 tablespoon lemon juice (or lime juice)
- Salt and black pepper to taste
- Optional: Feta cheese, crumbled (for garnish)

Instructions:

- Prepare the Vegetables:
    - Slice the cucumbers thinly. Dice the avocados and thinly slice the red onion. Chop the fresh cilantro and dill.
- Combine Ingredients:
    - In a large bowl, combine the sliced cucumbers, diced avocados, sliced red onion, chopped cilantro, and chopped dill.
- Make the Dressing:
    - In a small bowl, whisk together the extra-virgin olive oil and lemon (or lime) juice. Season with salt and black pepper to taste.
- Toss the Salad:
    - Pour the dressing over the cucumber and avocado mixture. Gently toss the salad until all ingredients are well coated with the dressing.
- Adjust Seasonings:
    - Taste the salad and adjust the salt and pepper as needed. You can also add more lemon juice or olive oil if desired.
- Chill (Optional):
    - If time allows, refrigerate the salad for about 15-30 minutes to let the flavors meld.
- Serve:
    - Serve the Cucumber and Avocado Salad as a side dish or a light and refreshing appetizer.
- Garnish (Optional):
    - Garnish with crumbled Feta cheese for an extra layer of flavor and creaminess.

This Cucumber and Avocado Salad is a perfect side dish for a barbecue, picnic, or as a light accompaniment to grilled meats or fish. It's a great way to enjoy the fresh flavors of summer. Enjoy!

Turkey and Vegetable Stir-Fry

Ingredients:

For the Stir-Fry Sauce:

- 3 tablespoons soy sauce
- 2 tablespoons oyster sauce
- 1 tablespoon hoisin sauce
- 1 tablespoon rice vinegar
- 1 tablespoon honey or maple syrup
- 1 teaspoon sesame oil
- 1 teaspoon cornstarch (optional, for thickening)

For the Stir-Fry:

- 1 pound ground turkey
- 2 tablespoons vegetable oil
- 3 cups mixed vegetables (broccoli, bell peppers, snap peas, carrots, etc.), chopped
- 3 cloves garlic, minced
- 1 tablespoon ginger, grated
- Cooked rice or noodles (for serving)

Optional Garnishes:

- Green onions, sliced
- Sesame seeds
- Crushed red pepper flakes

Instructions:

Prepare the Stir-Fry Sauce:

In a small bowl, whisk together soy sauce, oyster sauce, hoisin sauce, rice vinegar, honey (or maple syrup), sesame oil, and cornstarch (if using). Set aside.

Cook the Stir-Fry:

Heat vegetable oil in a wok or large skillet over medium-high heat.
Add ground turkey to the hot pan. Break it apart with a spatula and cook until browned and cooked through.
Add minced garlic and grated ginger to the turkey. Stir-fry for about 1-2 minutes until fragrant.

Add the mixed vegetables to the pan. Stir-fry for an additional 3-4 minutes until the vegetables are crisp-tender.

Pour the prepared stir-fry sauce over the turkey and vegetables. Toss everything together until well coated and heated through.

Taste and adjust the seasoning if needed. If you prefer a thicker sauce, you can cook for an additional 1-2 minutes to allow the cornstarch to thicken the sauce.

Serve:

Serve the turkey and vegetable stir-fry over cooked rice or noodles.

Garnish with sliced green onions, sesame seeds, and crushed red pepper flakes if desired.

This Turkey and Vegetable Stir-Fry is a versatile dish, and you can customize it with your favorite vegetables. It's a delicious and wholesome meal that comes together quickly, making it perfect for busy weeknights. Enjoy!

Roasted Brussels Sprouts with Balsamic Glaze

Ingredients:

- 1 pound Brussels sprouts, trimmed and halved
- 2 tablespoons olive oil
- Salt and black pepper to taste
- 2 tablespoons balsamic glaze (store-bought or homemade)
- 2 tablespoons grated Parmesan cheese (optional)
- Crushed red pepper flakes (optional, for heat)
- Chopped fresh parsley (for garnish)

Instructions:

Preheat the Oven:
- Preheat your oven to 400°F (200°C).

Prepare the Brussels Sprouts:
- Trim the ends of the Brussels sprouts and cut them in half.

Coat with Olive Oil:
- In a large bowl, toss the halved Brussels sprouts with olive oil, ensuring they are evenly coated. Season with salt and black pepper to taste.

Roast in the Oven:
- Spread the Brussels sprouts in a single layer on a baking sheet. Roast in the preheated oven for 20-25 minutes or until they are golden brown and crispy on the edges. Shake or stir the sprouts halfway through cooking for even browning.

Drizzle with Balsamic Glaze:
- Once the Brussels sprouts are roasted, transfer them to a serving dish. Drizzle balsamic glaze over the top.

Optional: Add Parmesan and Heat:
- Optionally, sprinkle grated Parmesan cheese over the Brussels sprouts for extra flavor. If you like a bit of heat, you can add crushed red pepper flakes as well.

Garnish and Serve:
- Garnish the roasted Brussels sprouts with chopped fresh parsley. Serve immediately.

This Roasted Brussels Sprouts with Balsamic Glaze dish is a wonderful combination of crispy, caramelized Brussels sprouts with the sweet and tangy flavor of balsamic glaze. It makes for a fantastic side dish that complements a variety of main courses. Enjoy!

Chickpea and Spinach Coconut Curry

Ingredients:

- 1 tablespoon coconut oil
- 1 large onion, finely chopped
- 3 cloves garlic, minced
- 1 tablespoon fresh ginger, grated
- 1 tablespoon curry powder
- 1 teaspoon ground cumin
- 1 teaspoon ground coriander
- 1/2 teaspoon turmeric
- 1/2 teaspoon cayenne pepper (adjust to taste)
- 1 can (15 oz) chickpeas, drained and rinsed
- 1 can (14 oz) diced tomatoes
- 1 can (14 oz) coconut milk
- 4 cups fresh spinach leaves, washed and chopped
- Salt and black pepper to taste
- Fresh cilantro, chopped (for garnish)
- Cooked rice or naan (for serving)

Instructions:

Saute Aromatics:
- In a large skillet or pot, heat coconut oil over medium heat. Add chopped onion and sauté until softened.

Add Garlic and Ginger:
- Add minced garlic and grated ginger to the skillet. Cook for about 1-2 minutes until fragrant.

Add Spices:
- Stir in curry powder, ground cumin, ground coriander, turmeric, and cayenne pepper. Cook for an additional 1-2 minutes to toast the spices.

Add Chickpeas and Tomatoes:
- Add drained chickpeas and diced tomatoes (with their juices) to the skillet. Stir well to combine.

Pour in Coconut Milk:
- Pour in coconut milk and bring the mixture to a simmer. Allow it to cook for 10-15 minutes to let the flavors meld.

Add Spinach:
- Add chopped spinach to the curry and stir until the spinach wilts.

Season:
- Season the curry with salt and black pepper to taste. Adjust the spice level if needed.

Garnish and Serve:
- Garnish the Chickpea and Spinach Coconut Curry with chopped fresh cilantro. Serve over cooked rice or with naan.

This Chickpea and Spinach Coconut Curry is a wholesome and flavorful plant-based meal. The combination of chickpeas, spinach, and coconut milk creates a creamy and satisfying curry. Enjoy this delicious dish for a quick and easy dinner!

Zucchini Noodles with Pesto and Cherry Tomatoes

Ingredients:

For the Pesto:

- 2 cups fresh basil leaves, packed
- 1/2 cup grated Parmesan cheese
- 1/2 cup pine nuts or walnuts
- 3 cloves garlic, peeled
- 1/2 cup extra-virgin olive oil
- Salt and black pepper to taste
- 1 tablespoon lemon juice (optional)

For the Zucchini Noodles:

- 4 medium-sized zucchini
- 1 tablespoon olive oil
- 1 pint cherry tomatoes, halved
- Salt and black pepper to taste
- Grated Parmesan cheese (for garnish)
- Pine nuts or chopped walnuts (for garnish)

Instructions:

Prepare the Pesto:

   Combine Ingredients:
   - In a food processor, combine basil, Parmesan cheese, pine nuts or walnuts, and garlic.

   Blend:
   - Pulse the ingredients until coarsely chopped. With the food processor running, gradually add the olive oil in a steady stream until the pesto reaches your desired consistency.

   Season:
   - Season the pesto with salt and black pepper to taste. Add lemon juice if desired for a hint of brightness.

Prepare the Zucchini Noodles:

   Make Zucchini Noodles:
   - Using a spiralizer, julienne peeler, or a knife, create zucchini noodles. If using a spiralizer, follow the manufacturer's instructions.

Cook Zucchini Noodles:
- Heat olive oil in a large skillet over medium heat. Add the zucchini noodles and cook for 2-3 minutes until just tender. Be careful not to overcook; you want the noodles to remain slightly crisp.

Add Cherry Tomatoes:
- Add halved cherry tomatoes to the skillet. Toss with the zucchini noodles and cook for an additional 1-2 minutes until the tomatoes are warmed through but still firm.

Combine with Pesto:
- Add the prepared pesto to the zucchini noodles and cherry tomatoes. Toss everything together until the noodles are evenly coated with the pesto.

Season:
- Season the dish with additional salt and black pepper if needed.

Serve:
- Divide the Zucchini Noodles with Pesto and Cherry Tomatoes among plates. Garnish with grated Parmesan cheese and pine nuts or chopped walnuts.

This Zucchini Noodles with Pesto and Cherry Tomatoes is a light, low-carb alternative to traditional pasta dishes. It's full of fresh flavors and can be enjoyed as a main course or a flavorful side dish. Enjoy!

Grilled Chicken with Mango Salsa

Ingredients:

For the Grilled Chicken:

- 4 boneless, skinless chicken breasts
- 2 tablespoons olive oil
- 1 teaspoon ground cumin
- 1 teaspoon smoked paprika
- 1 teaspoon garlic powder
- Salt and black pepper to taste
- Lime wedges (for serving)

For the Mango Salsa:

- 2 ripe mangoes, peeled, pitted, and diced
- 1/2 red onion, finely chopped
- 1 red bell pepper, diced
- 1 jalapeño, seeds removed and finely chopped
- 1/4 cup fresh cilantro, chopped
- Juice of 1 lime
- Salt to taste

Instructions:

Prepare the Grilled Chicken:

Marinate Chicken:
- In a bowl, mix olive oil, ground cumin, smoked paprika, garlic powder, salt, and black pepper. Coat the chicken breasts with the marinade and let them marinate for at least 30 minutes.

Preheat Grill:
- Preheat your grill to medium-high heat.

Grill Chicken:
- Grill the marinated chicken breasts for about 6-8 minutes per side or until they reach an internal temperature of 165°F (74°C) and have nice grill marks.

Rest and Slice:
- Allow the grilled chicken to rest for a few minutes before slicing it into strips.

Prepare the Mango Salsa:

Combine Ingredients:
- In a bowl, combine diced mangoes, chopped red onion, diced red bell pepper, chopped jalapeño, cilantro, and lime juice. Mix well.

Season:
- Season the mango salsa with salt to taste. Adjust the lime juice and salt according to your preference.

Serve:

Plate the Chicken:
- Arrange the grilled chicken strips on serving plates.

Top with Mango Salsa:
- Spoon the fresh mango salsa over the grilled chicken.

Garnish and Serve:
- Garnish with additional cilantro and serve with lime wedges on the side.

This Grilled Chicken with Mango Salsa is a perfect combination of smoky, savory chicken and the sweet, tangy flavors of the mango salsa. It's a vibrant and delicious dish that's great for outdoor gatherings or a light and refreshing dinner. Enjoy!

Quinoa Salad with Roasted Vegetables

Ingredients:

For the Roasted Vegetables:

- 2 cups cherry tomatoes, halved
- 1 medium zucchini, diced
- 1 red bell pepper, diced
- 1 yellow bell pepper, diced
- 1 red onion, diced
- 3 tablespoons olive oil
- 1 teaspoon dried oregano
- 1 teaspoon dried thyme
- Salt and black pepper to taste

For the Quinoa:

- 1 cup quinoa, rinsed
- 2 cups water or vegetable broth
- 1/4 cup fresh parsley, chopped
- 1/4 cup fresh basil, chopped

For the Dressing:

- 3 tablespoons olive oil
- 2 tablespoons balsamic vinegar
- 1 tablespoon Dijon mustard
- 1 clove garlic, minced
- Salt and black pepper to taste

Instructions:

Roast the Vegetables:

Preheat the Oven:
- Preheat your oven to 425°F (220°C).

Prepare Vegetables:
- In a large bowl, combine halved cherry tomatoes, diced zucchini, diced red and yellow bell peppers, and diced red onion.

Season and Toss:

- Drizzle olive oil over the vegetables and sprinkle with dried oregano, dried thyme, salt, and black pepper. Toss until the vegetables are evenly coated.

Roast:
- Spread the vegetables in a single layer on a baking sheet. Roast in the preheated oven for 20-25 minutes or until they are tender and slightly caramelized, stirring halfway through.

Cook Quinoa:

Rinse Quinoa:
- Rinse quinoa under cold water until the water runs clear.

Cook Quinoa:
- In a medium saucepan, combine quinoa and water or vegetable broth. Bring to a boil, then reduce the heat to low, cover, and simmer for 15-20 minutes or until the quinoa is cooked and the liquid is absorbed.

Fluff and Cool:
- Fluff the quinoa with a fork and let it cool to room temperature.

Prepare the Dressing:

Whisk Dressing:
- In a small bowl, whisk together olive oil, balsamic vinegar, Dijon mustard, minced garlic, salt, and black pepper.

Assemble the Salad:

Combine Ingredients:
- In a large bowl, combine the cooked and cooled quinoa, roasted vegetables, chopped fresh parsley, and chopped fresh basil.

Dress the Salad:
- Drizzle the dressing over the salad and toss gently until all the ingredients are well coated.

Serve:
- Serve the Quinoa Salad with Roasted Vegetables at room temperature or chilled. It's great on its own or as a side dish.

This Quinoa Salad with Roasted Vegetables is not only colorful and flavorful but also packed with protein and nutrients. It's a versatile dish that can be enjoyed year-round. Enjoy!

Baked Eggplant Parmesan

Ingredients:

For the Eggplant:

- 2 large eggplants, thinly sliced (about 1/4 inch thick)
- Salt, for sweating the eggplant
- 1 cup all-purpose flour
- 3 large eggs, beaten
- 2 cups breadcrumbs (Italian seasoned or plain)
- Olive oil cooking spray

For the Tomato Sauce:

- 2 cups marinara sauce (store-bought or homemade)
- 1 teaspoon dried oregano
- 1 teaspoon dried basil
- Salt and black pepper to taste

For the Cheese:

- 2 cups shredded mozzarella cheese
- 1/2 cup grated Parmesan cheese
- Fresh basil or parsley, chopped (for garnish)

Instructions:

Prepare the Eggplant:

Sweat the Eggplant:
- Sprinkle salt over the sliced eggplant and let it sit in a colander for about 30 minutes to draw out excess moisture. Rinse and pat dry.

Preheat Oven:
- Preheat your oven to 375°F (190°C).

Coat with Flour, Eggs, and Breadcrumbs:
- Set up a breading station with three shallow dishes. Place flour in one, beaten eggs in another, and breadcrumbs in the third. Dredge each eggplant slice in flour, dip in beaten eggs, and coat with breadcrumbs.

Bake the Eggplant:
- Place the breaded eggplant slices on a baking sheet lined with parchment paper. Spray the slices with olive oil cooking spray. Bake for 20-25 minutes or until the eggplant is golden brown and crispy.

Prepare the Tomato Sauce:

- Season the Sauce:
  - In a small saucepan, heat the marinara sauce over medium heat. Add dried oregano, dried basil, salt, and black pepper. Simmer for about 5-7 minutes to allow the flavors to meld.

Assemble and Bake:

- Layer the Eggplant:
  - In a baking dish, spread a thin layer of tomato sauce. Arrange a layer of baked eggplant slices over the sauce.
- Add Cheese:
  - Sprinkle a portion of shredded mozzarella and grated Parmesan over the eggplant layer.
- Repeat Layers:
  - Repeat the layers until all the eggplant slices are used, finishing with a generous layer of cheese on top.
- Bake:
  - Bake in the preheated oven for 25-30 minutes or until the cheese is melted and bubbly, and the edges are golden brown.
- Garnish and Serve:
  - Garnish with chopped fresh basil or parsley. Let it rest for a few minutes before slicing and serving.

This Baked Eggplant Parmesan is a wholesome and flavorful dish that captures the essence of the classic without the deep-frying. Serve it over pasta, with a side salad, or on its own for a satisfying meal. Enjoy!

Shrimp and Broccoli Stir-Fry

Ingredients:

For the Stir-Fry Sauce:

- 3 tablespoons soy sauce
- 2 tablespoons oyster sauce
- 1 tablespoon hoisin sauce
- 1 tablespoon rice vinegar
- 1 tablespoon honey or maple syrup
- 1 teaspoon sesame oil
- 1 teaspoon cornstarch (optional, for thickening)

For the Stir-Fry:

- 1 pound large shrimp, peeled and deveined
- 2 tablespoons vegetable oil
- 4 cups broccoli florets
- 3 cloves garlic, minced
- 1 tablespoon fresh ginger, grated
- Cooked rice or noodles (for serving)
- Sesame seeds and chopped green onions (for garnish)

Instructions:

Prepare the Stir-Fry Sauce:

Combine Ingredients:
- In a small bowl, whisk together soy sauce, oyster sauce, hoisin sauce, rice vinegar, honey (or maple syrup), sesame oil, and cornstarch (if using). Set aside.

Prepare the Shrimp and Broccoli:

Prep Shrimp:
- Pat the shrimp dry with paper towels. Season with salt and black pepper.

Blanch Broccoli:
- Blanch the broccoli florets in boiling water for 2 minutes, then transfer them to an ice bath to stop the cooking process. Drain and set aside.

Cook the Stir-Fry:

Heat Oil:

- Heat vegetable oil in a large wok or skillet over medium-high heat.

Cook Shrimp:
- Add the shrimp to the hot pan and cook for 2-3 minutes on each side until they turn pink and opaque. Remove shrimp from the pan and set aside.

Cook Aromatics:
- In the same pan, add a bit more oil if needed. Add minced garlic and grated ginger. Stir-fry for about 30 seconds until fragrant.

Stir-Fry Broccoli:
- Add the blanched broccoli florets to the pan. Stir-fry for 2-3 minutes until they are tender-crisp.

Combine with Shrimp:
- Return the cooked shrimp to the pan with the broccoli.

Pour in Sauce:
- Pour the prepared stir-fry sauce over the shrimp and broccoli. Toss everything together until well coated and heated through.

Adjust Seasonings:
- Taste and adjust the seasoning if needed. If you prefer a thicker sauce, you can cook for an additional 1-2 minutes to allow the cornstarch to thicken.

Serve:

Serve Over Rice or Noodles:
- Serve the Shrimp and Broccoli Stir-Fry over cooked rice or noodles.

Garnish:
- Garnish with sesame seeds and chopped green onions before serving.

This Shrimp and Broccoli Stir-Fry is a quick and tasty meal that's perfect for busy weeknights. It's a well-balanced dish with a delicious combination of shrimp, broccoli, and a savory stir-fry sauce. Enjoy!

Greek Salad with Feta and Olives

Ingredients:

For the Salad:

- 4 cups cherry tomatoes, halved
- 1 cucumber, diced
- 1 red bell pepper, diced
- 1 yellow bell pepper, diced
- 1 red onion, thinly sliced
- 1 cup Kalamata olives, pitted
- 1 cup crumbled feta cheese
- 1 cup cucumber, diced
- 1 cup red cherry tomatoes, halved
- 1/2 cup red onion, thinly sliced
- 1/4 cup fresh parsley, chopped
- 1/4 cup fresh mint, chopped (optional)

For the Dressing:

- 1/4 cup extra-virgin olive oil
- 2 tablespoons red wine vinegar
- 1 teaspoon dried oregano
- Salt and black pepper to taste

Instructions:

Prepare the Salad:

   Combine Vegetables:
   - In a large bowl, combine cherry tomatoes, diced cucumber, diced red and yellow bell peppers, sliced red onion, olives, crumbled feta cheese, fresh parsley, and fresh mint.

Prepare the Dressing:

   Whisk Dressing:
   - In a small bowl, whisk together extra-virgin olive oil, red wine vinegar, dried oregano, salt, and black pepper. Adjust the seasoning to taste.

Assemble the Greek Salad:

- Pour Dressing:
    - Pour the dressing over the salad ingredients.
- Toss Gently:
    - Gently toss the salad until all the ingredients are well coated with the dressing.
- Chill (Optional):
    - If time allows, refrigerate the salad for about 15-30 minutes to let the flavors meld.
- Serve:
    - Serve the Greek Salad with Feta and Olives as a refreshing side dish or add grilled chicken or shrimp for a complete meal.

This Greek Salad is a delightful combination of crisp vegetables, briny olives, and creamy feta, all brought together with a zesty dressing. It's perfect for a light lunch, a side dish at a barbecue, or as a refreshing salad for warm days. Enjoy!

Teriyaki Tofu Lettuce Wraps

Ingredients:

For the Teriyaki Tofu:

- 1 block extra-firm tofu, pressed and cubed
- 1/4 cup soy sauce
- 2 tablespoons teriyaki sauce
- 1 tablespoon maple syrup or honey
- 1 tablespoon rice vinegar
- 1 teaspoon sesame oil
- 1 teaspoon fresh ginger, grated
- 2 cloves garlic, minced
- 1 tablespoon cornstarch mixed with 2 tablespoons water (for thickening)
- Sesame seeds (for garnish)

For the Lettuce Wraps:

- Large lettuce leaves (such as iceberg or butter lettuce)
- Cooked rice or quinoa (optional, for serving)
- Sliced green onions (for garnish)
- Sliced radishes (for garnish)
- Fresh cilantro or mint leaves (for garnish)

Instructions:

Prepare the Teriyaki Tofu:

Press Tofu:
- Press the tofu to remove excess water. You can use a tofu press or wrap the tofu block in a clean kitchen towel and place something heavy on top for about 15-20 minutes.

Marinate Tofu:
- In a bowl, whisk together soy sauce, teriyaki sauce, maple syrup or honey, rice vinegar, sesame oil, grated ginger, and minced garlic. Add the cubed tofu to the marinade and let it marinate for at least 30 minutes.

Cook Tofu:
- In a non-stick skillet or wok, cook the marinated tofu over medium-high heat until golden brown and slightly crispy.

Add Cornstarch Mixture:

- Pour the cornstarch mixture over the tofu and toss to coat. Cook for an additional 1-2 minutes until the sauce thickens.

Garnish:
- Sprinkle sesame seeds over the tofu and toss to coat. Remove from heat.

Assemble the Lettuce Wraps:

Prepare Lettuce Leaves:
- Carefully separate the leaves of the lettuce to create cups for the filling.

Add Tofu:
- Spoon the teriyaki tofu into each lettuce cup.

Add Toppings:
- Add cooked rice or quinoa (if using) to each cup. Top with sliced green onions, sliced radishes, and fresh cilantro or mint leaves.

Serve:
- Serve the Teriyaki Tofu Lettuce Wraps immediately. Enjoy them as a light and flavorful meal or appetizer.

These Teriyaki Tofu Lettuce Wraps are not only delicious but also packed with protein and vibrant flavors. Customize the toppings to suit your taste, and enjoy a satisfying and healthy meal!

Cauliflower Fried Rice

Ingredients:

- 1 medium-sized cauliflower
- 2 tablespoons vegetable oil
- 1 cup diced carrots
- 1 cup frozen peas
- 1/2 cup diced bell peppers (any color)
- 1/2 cup diced onion
- 2 cloves garlic, minced
- 2 eggs, beaten
- 3 tablespoons soy sauce (or tamari for a gluten-free option)
- 1 tablespoon sesame oil
- Green onions, chopped, for garnish
- Sesame seeds, for garnish (optional)

Instructions:

Prepare the Cauliflower Rice:

Rice the Cauliflower:
- Cut the cauliflower into florets. Place the florets in a food processor and pulse until it resembles the texture of rice. You may need to do this in batches.

Cook Cauliflower Rice:
- Heat a large skillet or wok over medium heat. Add 1 tablespoon of vegetable oil. Stir in the cauliflower rice and cook for 5-7 minutes, stirring occasionally, until it becomes tender but not mushy. Remove the cauliflower rice from the skillet and set aside.

Cook the Fried Rice:

Sauté Vegetables:
- In the same skillet, add the remaining 1 tablespoon of vegetable oil. Add diced carrots, frozen peas, diced bell peppers, and diced onion. Sauté for about 5 minutes until the vegetables are tender-crisp.

Add Garlic:
- Add minced garlic to the vegetables and sauté for an additional 1-2 minutes until fragrant.

Push Vegetables to the Side:
- Push the vegetables to one side of the skillet, creating a space to cook the eggs.

Cook Eggs:
- Pour the beaten eggs into the empty space and scramble them. Once the eggs are cooked, mix them with the sautéed vegetables.

Combine with Cauliflower Rice:
- Add the cooked cauliflower rice back into the skillet with the vegetables and eggs. Mix everything together.

Season with Soy Sauce and Sesame Oil:
- Pour soy sauce and sesame oil over the cauliflower rice mixture. Stir well to combine and evenly distribute the flavors.

Adjust Seasoning:
- Taste the cauliflower fried rice and adjust the seasoning if needed. You can add more soy sauce or salt according to your preference.

Garnish and Serve:
- Garnish with chopped green onions and sesame seeds if desired. Serve the cauliflower fried rice hot.

This Cauliflower Fried Rice is a tasty and satisfying dish that's perfect for those looking for a low-carb or gluten-free option. It's a versatile recipe, and you can customize it by adding your favorite protein, such as tofu, chicken, or shrimp. Enjoy!

Black Bean and Corn Salsa

Ingredients:

- 1 can (15 oz) black beans, drained and rinsed
- 1 cup frozen corn kernels, thawed
- 1 cup cherry tomatoes, diced
- 1/2 red onion, finely chopped
- 1/4 cup fresh cilantro, chopped
- 1 jalapeño, seeds removed and finely chopped
- 2 cloves garlic, minced
- Juice of 1 lime
- 2 tablespoons olive oil
- 1 teaspoon ground cumin
- Salt and black pepper to taste
- Avocado slices for garnish (optional)

Instructions:

Combine Ingredients:
- In a large bowl, combine black beans, corn, diced cherry tomatoes, chopped red onion, chopped cilantro, chopped jalapeño, and minced garlic.

Prepare Dressing:
- In a small bowl, whisk together lime juice, olive oil, ground cumin, salt, and black pepper.

Toss and Coat:
- Pour the dressing over the black bean and corn mixture. Toss everything together until well coated with the dressing.

Chill (Optional):
- If time allows, refrigerate the salsa for about 30 minutes to let the flavors meld. This step is optional, and you can serve it immediately if you prefer.

Garnish and Serve:
- Garnish the black bean and corn salsa with avocado slices if desired. Serve as a dip with tortilla chips, as a topping for tacos, or as a side salad.

This Black Bean and Corn Salsa is not only delicious but also packed with protein, fiber, and fresh flavors. It's a versatile dish that adds a burst of color and taste to your meals.

Enjoy!

Lemon Garlic Roasted Shrimp

Ingredients:

- 1 pound large shrimp, peeled and deveined
- 3 tablespoons olive oil
- 4 cloves garlic, minced
- Zest of 1 lemon
- Juice of 1 lemon
- 1 teaspoon dried oregano
- 1 teaspoon paprika
- 1/2 teaspoon red pepper flakes (optional)
- Salt and black pepper to taste
- Fresh parsley, chopped (for garnish)

Instructions:

Preheat Oven:
- Preheat your oven to 400°F (200°C).

Prepare Shrimp:
- In a large bowl, toss the peeled and deveined shrimp with olive oil, minced garlic, lemon zest, lemon juice, dried oregano, paprika, red pepper flakes (if using), salt, and black pepper. Ensure that the shrimp are well-coated with the marinade.

Marinate:
- Allow the shrimp to marinate for at least 15-20 minutes to absorb the flavors.

Arrange on Baking Sheet:
- Line a baking sheet with parchment paper. Arrange the marinated shrimp in a single layer on the baking sheet.

Roast in the Oven:
- Roast the shrimp in the preheated oven for 8-10 minutes or until they are pink and opaque, with slightly crispy edges.

Broil (Optional):
- If you like, you can broil the shrimp for an additional 1-2 minutes to give them a touch of extra color and flavor.

Garnish and Serve:
- Sprinkle chopped fresh parsley over the roasted shrimp. Serve them hot as an appetizer or main course.

Lemon Garlic Roasted Shrimp is versatile and pairs well with various sides such as rice, pasta, or a crisp green salad. It's a quick and easy recipe that brings out the natural flavors of the shrimp with the zesty combination of lemon and garlic. Enjoy!

Turkey and Sweet Potato Chili

Ingredients:

- 1 tablespoon olive oil
- 1 onion, diced
- 1 bell pepper (any color), diced
- 3 cloves garlic, minced
- 1 pound ground turkey
- 2 medium sweet potatoes, peeled and diced
- 1 can (15 oz) black beans, drained and rinsed
- 1 can (15 oz) diced tomatoes
- 1 can (6 oz) tomato paste
- 2 cups chicken or vegetable broth
- 1 tablespoon chili powder
- 1 teaspoon cumin
- 1 teaspoon paprika
- 1/2 teaspoon cinnamon
- Salt and black pepper to taste
- Optional toppings: shredded cheese, sour cream, chopped green onions, cilantro

Instructions:

Sauté Vegetables:
- In a large pot or Dutch oven, heat olive oil over medium heat. Add diced onion and bell pepper. Sauté until softened, about 5 minutes.

Add Garlic and Turkey:
- Add minced garlic and ground turkey to the pot. Cook until the turkey is browned, breaking it apart with a spoon as it cooks.

Add Sweet Potatoes:
- Stir in the diced sweet potatoes and cook for 3-4 minutes.

Season and Add Ingredients:
- Add chili powder, cumin, paprika, cinnamon, salt, and black pepper. Stir well to coat the ingredients. Add black beans, diced tomatoes, tomato paste, and chicken or vegetable broth.

Simmer:
- Bring the chili to a simmer. Reduce the heat to low, cover, and let it simmer for about 20-25 minutes or until the sweet potatoes are tender.

Adjust Seasoning:

- Taste the chili and adjust the seasoning if needed. Add more salt, pepper, or spices according to your preference.

Serve:
- Ladle the Turkey and Sweet Potato Chili into bowls. Top with optional toppings such as shredded cheese, sour cream, chopped green onions, or cilantro.

Turkey and Sweet Potato Chili is a comforting and nutritious meal that combines the sweetness of sweet potatoes with the savory flavors of turkey and spices. It's a great one-pot dish that can be easily customized to suit your taste. Enjoy!

Caprese Salad with Balsamic Glaze

Ingredients:

- 4 large ripe tomatoes, sliced
- 1 pound fresh mozzarella cheese, sliced
- Fresh basil leaves
- Balsamic glaze
- Extra-virgin olive oil
- Salt and black pepper to taste

Instructions:

Assemble the Salad:
- Arrange the tomato slices and mozzarella cheese slices on a serving platter, alternating them and slightly overlapping. Tuck fresh basil leaves between the tomato and mozzarella slices.

Season:
- Sprinkle salt and black pepper over the tomato and mozzarella slices. The amount of salt can be adjusted based on your preference.

Drizzle with Olive Oil:
- Drizzle extra-virgin olive oil over the salad. The olive oil adds richness and enhances the flavors.

Balsamic Glaze:
- Drizzle balsamic glaze generously over the Caprese salad. The balsamic glaze adds sweetness and acidity, complementing the fresh ingredients.

Serve:
- Serve the Caprese Salad with Balsamic Glaze immediately as a refreshing appetizer or side dish.

This Caprese Salad is a delightful combination of juicy tomatoes, creamy mozzarella, and aromatic basil, all brought together with the sweet and tangy balsamic glaze. It's a perfect dish for summer when tomatoes are at their peak. Enjoy!

Pesto Zoodles with Cherry Tomatoes

Ingredients:

- 4 medium-sized zucchini, spiralized into noodles
- 1 cup cherry tomatoes, halved
- 1/2 cup fresh basil leaves, chopped
- 1/3 cup pine nuts, toasted
- 1/2 cup grated Parmesan cheese
- 2 cloves garlic, minced
- 1/2 cup extra-virgin olive oil
- Salt and black pepper to taste
- Red pepper flakes (optional, for some heat)

Instructions:

Prepare Zoodles:
- Spiralize the zucchini into noodles using a spiralizer. If you don't have a spiralizer, you can use a vegetable peeler to create wide ribbons.

Toast Pine Nuts:
- In a dry skillet over medium heat, toast the pine nuts until they are golden brown. Be careful not to burn them. Set aside.

Make Pesto:
- In a food processor, combine the chopped basil, toasted pine nuts, grated Parmesan, minced garlic, and a pinch of salt. Pulse until the ingredients are finely chopped.

Add Olive Oil:
- With the food processor running, slowly drizzle in the extra-virgin olive oil until the pesto reaches your desired consistency. You may need to scrape down the sides of the processor bowl.

Season and Adjust:
- Taste the pesto and add salt and black pepper as needed. If you like some heat, you can add red pepper flakes.

Toss Zoodles:
- In a large bowl, toss the zucchini noodles with the pesto until well coated.

Add Cherry Tomatoes:
- Gently fold in the halved cherry tomatoes, distributing them evenly.

Serve:
- Serve the Pesto Zoodles with Cherry Tomatoes immediately. You can garnish with extra Parmesan and basil if desired.

Pesto Zoodles with Cherry Tomatoes is a quick and healthy dish that showcases the freshness of the ingredients. It's a great option for a light lunch or dinner, especially during the warmer months. Enjoy!

Salmon and Asparagus Foil Packets

Ingredients:

- 4 salmon fillets
- 1 bunch of asparagus, trimmed
- 1 lemon, thinly sliced
- 4 cloves garlic, minced
- 4 tablespoons butter, divided
- 2 tablespoons fresh dill, chopped
- Salt and black pepper to taste
- Olive oil (for drizzling)

Instructions:

Preheat Oven:
- Preheat your oven to 400°F (200°C).

Prepare Foil Packets:
- Tear four sheets of aluminum foil, each large enough to wrap one salmon fillet and some asparagus. Place a salmon fillet in the center of each piece of foil.

Season Salmon:
- Season each salmon fillet with salt and black pepper to taste.

Add Asparagus:
- Arrange a handful of trimmed asparagus around each salmon fillet.

Add Lemon and Garlic:
- Place lemon slices on top of each salmon fillet and distribute minced garlic evenly among the packets.

Dot with Butter:
- Add 1 tablespoon of butter to each foil packet. Drizzle each packet with a bit of olive oil.

Sprinkle with Dill:
- Sprinkle fresh dill over the salmon and asparagus.

Seal Packets:
- Fold the sides of the foil over the salmon and asparagus, sealing the edges tightly to create a packet.

Bake:
- Place the foil packets on a baking sheet and bake in the preheated oven for 15-20 minutes, or until the salmon is cooked through and flakes easily with a fork.

Serve:
- Carefully open the foil packets, and serve the Salmon and Asparagus with lemon slices on top. You can also squeeze additional fresh lemon juice if desired.

These Salmon and Asparagus Foil Packets are not only delicious but also convenient for a quick weeknight dinner. The ingredients cook together, infusing the salmon and asparagus with delightful flavors. Enjoy this simple and healthy meal!

Mediterranean Chickpea Quinoa Bowl

Ingredients:

For the Quinoa:

- 1 cup quinoa, rinsed
- 2 cups vegetable broth or water
- 1/2 teaspoon salt

For the Chickpeas:

- 1 can (15 oz) chickpeas, drained and rinsed
- 1 tablespoon olive oil
- 1 teaspoon ground cumin
- 1 teaspoon paprika
- Salt and black pepper to taste

For the Bowl:

- Cherry tomatoes, halved
- Cucumber, diced
- Kalamata olives, sliced
- Red onion, thinly sliced
- Feta cheese, crumbled
- Fresh parsley, chopped

For the Dressing:

- 1/4 cup extra-virgin olive oil
- 2 tablespoons red wine vinegar
- 1 teaspoon dried oregano
- Salt and black pepper to taste

Instructions:

Prepare Quinoa:

　　Cook Quinoa:
- In a medium saucepan, combine quinoa, vegetable broth or water, and salt. Bring to a boil, then reduce heat to low, cover, and simmer for about 15 minutes or until the quinoa is cooked and liquid is absorbed. Fluff with a fork.

Roast Chickpeas:

- Preheat Oven:
  - Preheat your oven to 400°F (200°C).
- Toss Chickpeas:
  - In a bowl, toss the drained and rinsed chickpeas with olive oil, ground cumin, paprika, salt, and black pepper.
- Roast Chickpeas:
  - Spread the seasoned chickpeas on a baking sheet and roast in the preheated oven for about 20-25 minutes, or until they are crispy and golden brown.

Prepare Dressing:

- Whisk Dressing:
  - In a small bowl, whisk together extra-virgin olive oil, red wine vinegar, dried oregano, salt, and black pepper.

Assemble the Bowl:

- Build Base:
  - In serving bowls, start with a base of cooked quinoa.
- Add Chickpeas:
  - Top the quinoa with the roasted chickpeas.
- Add Fresh Vegetables:
  - Arrange cherry tomatoes, diced cucumber, sliced Kalamata olives, and thinly sliced red onion over the quinoa and chickpeas.
- Add Feta and Parsley:
  - Sprinkle crumbled feta cheese and chopped fresh parsley over the bowl.
- Drizzle with Dressing:
  - Drizzle the prepared dressing over the Mediterranean Chickpea Quinoa Bowl.
- Serve:
  - Toss everything together or serve it as is, allowing individuals to mix their own bowls.

This Mediterranean Chickpea Quinoa Bowl is a well-balanced and satisfying meal that is rich in protein, fiber, and a variety of flavors. It's a perfect option for a healthy and delicious lunch or dinner. Enjoy!

Broccoli and Cheddar Stuffed Chicken Breast

Ingredients:

- 4 boneless, skinless chicken breasts
- Salt and black pepper to taste
- 1 teaspoon garlic powder
- 1 teaspoon onion powder
- 1 teaspoon smoked paprika
- 1 cup broccoli florets, steamed and chopped
- 1 cup shredded cheddar cheese
- 1 tablespoon olive oil
- 1 cup chicken broth (for baking)

Instructions:

Preheat Oven:
- Preheat your oven to 375°F (190°C).

Prepare Chicken Breasts:
- Season the chicken breasts with salt, black pepper, garlic powder, onion powder, and smoked paprika. Use a sharp knife to cut a pocket into the side of each chicken breast, being careful not to cut all the way through.

Stuff with Broccoli and Cheddar:
- In a bowl, mix together the chopped broccoli and shredded cheddar cheese. Stuff each chicken breast pocket with the broccoli and cheddar mixture.

Secure with Toothpicks:
- Use toothpicks to secure the edges of the chicken breasts, closing the pockets and preventing the filling from oozing out.

Sear Chicken:
- In an oven-safe skillet, heat olive oil over medium-high heat. Sear the stuffed chicken breasts for 2-3 minutes on each side until they are golden brown.

Add Chicken Broth:
- Pour chicken broth into the skillet around the chicken breasts. This helps keep the chicken moist during baking.

Bake:
- Transfer the skillet to the preheated oven and bake for 25-30 minutes or until the internal temperature of the chicken reaches 165°F (74°C).

Rest and Serve:

- Remove the toothpicks from the chicken breasts and let them rest for a few minutes before serving.

Optional Broil (Crispy Top):
- If you want a crispy top, you can broil the chicken for 1-2 minutes after baking.

Serve:
- Serve the Broccoli and Cheddar Stuffed Chicken Breast with your favorite sides, such as steamed vegetables, rice, or a fresh salad.

This dish combines the tenderness of chicken with the creamy texture of melted cheddar and the freshness of broccoli. It's a comforting and satisfying meal that's perfect for a family dinner or special occasion. Enjoy!

Butternut Squash and Lentil Soup

Ingredients:

- 1 tablespoon olive oil
- 1 onion, chopped
- 2 cloves garlic, minced
- 1 butternut squash, peeled, seeded, and diced (about 4 cups)
- 1 cup dried red lentils, rinsed and drained
- 4 cups vegetable broth
- 1 teaspoon ground cumin
- 1/2 teaspoon ground coriander
- 1/2 teaspoon smoked paprika
- 1/4 teaspoon cayenne pepper (optional, for heat)
- Salt and black pepper to taste
- Juice of 1 lemon
- Fresh cilantro or parsley, chopped (for garnish)
- Greek yogurt or coconut milk (for serving, optional)

Instructions:

Sauté Onion and Garlic:
- In a large pot, heat olive oil over medium heat. Add chopped onion and sauté until translucent, about 3-4 minutes. Add minced garlic and sauté for an additional 1-2 minutes.

Add Butternut Squash:
- Add diced butternut squash to the pot and cook for 5 minutes, stirring occasionally.

Add Lentils and Spices:
- Stir in the red lentils, ground cumin, ground coriander, smoked paprika, and cayenne pepper (if using). Cook for 1-2 minutes to toast the spices.

Pour in Vegetable Broth:
- Pour the vegetable broth into the pot. Bring the soup to a boil, then reduce the heat to low, cover, and simmer for about 20-25 minutes or until the lentils and butternut squash are tender.

Season and Blend (Optional):
- Season the soup with salt and black pepper to taste. If you prefer a smoother texture, you can use an immersion blender to blend part of the soup, leaving some chunks for texture.

Add Lemon Juice:

- Stir in the lemon juice to brighten the flavors. Adjust the seasoning if needed.

Serve:
- Ladle the Butternut Squash and Lentil Soup into bowls. Garnish with chopped fresh cilantro or parsley. You can also swirl in a spoonful of Greek yogurt or coconut milk before serving.

Enjoy:
- Serve the soup hot and enjoy the warm and comforting flavors.

This Butternut Squash and Lentil Soup is not only delicious but also rich in fiber and nutrients. It's a wholesome and filling soup that makes a perfect meal on its own or paired with crusty bread. Enjoy!

Chicken and Vegetable Skewers

Ingredients:

- 1.5 pounds boneless, skinless chicken breasts, cut into cubes
- 1 bell pepper, cut into chunks (any color)
- 1 zucchini, sliced into rounds
- 1 red onion, cut into chunks
- Cherry tomatoes
- Olive oil
- 3 cloves garlic, minced
- 1 teaspoon dried oregano
- 1 teaspoon dried thyme
- Salt and black pepper to taste
- Lemon wedges (for serving, optional)
- Wooden or metal skewers

Instructions:

Marinate the Chicken:
- In a bowl, combine the chicken cubes with olive oil, minced garlic, dried oregano, dried thyme, salt, and black pepper. Toss to coat the chicken evenly and let it marinate for at least 30 minutes.

Prepare the Skewers:
- If using wooden skewers, soak them in water for about 30 minutes to prevent them from burning during cooking. Thread the marinated chicken, bell peppers, zucchini, red onions, and cherry tomatoes onto the skewers, alternating between the ingredients.

Preheat Grill or Oven:
- Preheat your grill or oven to medium-high heat.

Grill or Bake:
- If grilling: Place the skewers on the preheated grill. Grill for about 10-15 minutes, turning occasionally, until the chicken is cooked through and has a nice char.
- If baking: Preheat the oven to 400°F (200°C). Place the skewers on a lined baking sheet and bake for about 20-25 minutes or until the chicken is fully cooked.

Serve:

- Remove the skewers from the grill or oven. Squeeze fresh lemon juice over the skewers if desired. Serve the chicken and vegetable skewers hot, either on their own or with your favorite side dishes.

Enjoy:
- Enjoy these flavorful and juicy chicken and vegetable skewers!

These chicken and vegetable skewers are versatile, and you can customize the vegetables and seasonings to suit your taste. They make a great addition to any barbecue or dinner party. Serve them with rice, couscous, or a refreshing salad for a complete meal. Enjoy!

Brussels Sprouts and Bacon Hash

Ingredients:

- 1 pound Brussels sprouts, trimmed and halved
- 6 slices bacon, chopped
- 1 onion, finely chopped
- 2 cloves garlic, minced
- 1/2 teaspoon red pepper flakes (optional, for some heat)
- Salt and black pepper to taste
- 1 tablespoon olive oil
- 1 tablespoon balsamic vinegar (optional, for added flavor)
- Chopped fresh parsley (for garnish)

Instructions:

Prepare Brussels Sprouts:
- Trim the ends of the Brussels sprouts and cut them in half.

Cook Bacon:
- In a large skillet over medium heat, cook the chopped bacon until it becomes crispy. Remove bacon from the skillet and set it aside on a paper towel-lined plate.

Sauté Vegetables:
- In the same skillet, add olive oil. Sauté the finely chopped onion until it becomes translucent, about 3-4 minutes. Add minced garlic and red pepper flakes (if using), and sauté for an additional 1-2 minutes.

Cook Brussels Sprouts:
- Add the halved Brussels sprouts to the skillet. Season with salt and black pepper. Cook, stirring occasionally, until the Brussels sprouts are tender and slightly caramelized, about 8-10 minutes.

Combine with Bacon:
- Return the cooked bacon to the skillet and toss everything together. Cook for an additional 2-3 minutes to heat the bacon and allow the flavors to meld.

Add Balsamic Vinegar (Optional):
- If using balsamic vinegar, drizzle it over the Brussels sprouts and bacon. Toss to combine and cook for an additional 1-2 minutes.

Garnish and Serve:
- Garnish the Brussels Sprouts and Bacon Hash with chopped fresh parsley. Serve hot as a side dish or a flavorful topping for breakfast dishes.

Enjoy:
- Enjoy the delicious combination of crispy bacon, caramelized Brussels sprouts, and savory flavors!

This Brussels Sprouts and Bacon Hash is a versatile dish that works well as a side for dinner or as part of a hearty breakfast. The addition of balsamic vinegar adds a touch of sweetness and acidity to balance the richness of the bacon. Enjoy!

Quinoa and Kale Patties

Ingredients:

- 1 cup quinoa, cooked and cooled
- 2 cups kale, finely chopped
- 1/2 cup breadcrumbs (whole wheat or gluten-free)
- 1/2 cup grated Parmesan cheese (optional, for non-vegan version)
- 3 cloves garlic, minced
- 1/2 cup red onion, finely chopped
- 2 tablespoons fresh parsley, chopped
- 2 tablespoons flaxseed meal (mixed with 6 tablespoons water, to replace eggs)
- 1 teaspoon cumin
- 1/2 teaspoon paprika
- Salt and black pepper to taste
- Olive oil for cooking

Instructions:

Prepare Flaxseed "Eggs":
- In a small bowl, mix the flaxseed meal with water and let it sit for 5-10 minutes until it thickens, creating a flaxseed "egg" substitute.

Cook Quinoa:
- Cook the quinoa according to the package instructions. Once cooked, allow it to cool.

Sauté Kale:
- In a skillet, sauté the finely chopped kale over medium heat until wilted. This should take about 3-5 minutes. Set aside to cool.

Combine Ingredients:
- In a large mixing bowl, combine the cooked quinoa, sautéed kale, breadcrumbs, Parmesan cheese (if using), minced garlic, chopped red onion, fresh parsley, flaxseed "eggs," cumin, paprika, salt, and black pepper. Mix well until all ingredients are evenly combined.

Form Patties:
- Take a portion of the mixture and shape it into a patty. Repeat until all the mixture is used.

Cook Patties:
- Heat olive oil in a skillet over medium heat. Cook the quinoa and kale patties for about 3-4 minutes on each side, or until golden brown and crispy.

Serve:
- Once cooked, transfer the patties to a serving plate. Serve them hot with your favorite dipping sauce or as a topping for salads or grain bowls.

Enjoy:
- Enjoy these nutritious and flavorful Quinoa and Kale Patties as a tasty and satisfying vegetarian or vegan meal!

These patties are versatile and can be enjoyed in various ways, such as on a bun as a burger, in a wrap, or on top of a salad. Feel free to customize the recipe by adding your favorite herbs and spices. Enjoy!

Baked Cod with Tomato and Olive Tapenade

Ingredients:

- 4 cod fillets
- Salt and black pepper to taste
- 2 tablespoons olive oil
- 1 pint cherry tomatoes, halved
- 1/2 cup Kalamata olives, pitted and chopped
- 2 tablespoons capers, drained
- 2 cloves garlic, minced
- 1 tablespoon fresh basil, chopped
- 1 tablespoon fresh parsley, chopped
- 1 tablespoon fresh lemon juice
- Lemon wedges (for serving)
- Optional: Crushed red pepper flakes for some heat

Instructions:

Preheat Oven:
- Preheat your oven to 400°F (200°C).

Season Cod Fillets:
- Season the cod fillets with salt and black pepper. Place them in a baking dish.

Prepare Tapenade:
- In a bowl, combine halved cherry tomatoes, chopped olives, capers, minced garlic, fresh basil, fresh parsley, fresh lemon juice, and olive oil. Mix well. If you like some heat, you can add a pinch of crushed red pepper flakes.

Top Cod with Tapenade:
- Spoon the tomato and olive tapenade over the cod fillets, ensuring they are evenly coated.

Bake:
- Bake in the preheated oven for about 15-20 minutes or until the cod is cooked through and flakes easily with a fork.

Serve:
- Once baked, remove the cod from the oven. Serve the Baked Cod with Tomato and Olive Tapenade hot, garnished with additional fresh herbs if desired, and lemon wedges on the side.

Enjoy:

- Enjoy this flavorful and Mediterranean-inspired dish!

This Baked Cod with Tomato and Olive Tapenade is not only delicious but also a healthy and low-carb option. The combination of tomatoes, olives, and capers adds a burst of flavors that perfectly complements the mild taste of the cod. It's a quick and impressive dish for any occasion. Enjoy!

Roasted Red Pepper and Chickpea Wrap

Ingredients:

For the Roasted Red Peppers and Chickpeas:

- 1 can (15 oz) chickpeas, drained and rinsed
- 2 large red bell peppers, thinly sliced
- 2 tablespoons olive oil
- 1 teaspoon ground cumin
- 1 teaspoon smoked paprika
- Salt and black pepper to taste

For the Tahini Dressing:

- 1/4 cup tahini
- 2 tablespoons lemon juice
- 1 tablespoon olive oil
- 1 clove garlic, minced
- 1 tablespoon chopped fresh parsley
- Salt and black pepper to taste
- Water (to thin the dressing, if needed)

For the Wrap:

- Whole-grain wraps or tortillas
- Fresh spinach or lettuce
- Sliced cucumber
- Sliced red onion
- Hummus (optional, for spreading)

Instructions:

Roasted Red Peppers and Chickpeas:

  Preheat Oven:
  - Preheat your oven to 400°F (200°C).

  Prepare Chickpeas and Peppers:
  - In a bowl, toss the chickpeas and thinly sliced red bell peppers with olive oil, ground cumin, smoked paprika, salt, and black pepper.

  Roast:

- Spread the chickpeas and peppers on a baking sheet in a single layer. Roast in the preheated oven for about 20-25 minutes or until the chickpeas are crispy and the peppers are tender.

Tahini Dressing:
- While the chickpeas and peppers are roasting, prepare the tahini dressing. In a bowl, whisk together tahini, lemon juice, olive oil, minced garlic, chopped fresh parsley, salt, and black pepper. If the dressing is too thick, you can thin it with a little water.

Assembling the Wrap:

Warm Wraps:
- If desired, warm the whole-grain wraps or tortillas according to the package instructions.

Spread Hummus (Optional):
- If using hummus, spread a layer on each wrap.

Layer with Spinach, Cucumber, and Red Onion:
- Place a handful of fresh spinach or lettuce on each wrap. Top with sliced cucumber and red onion.

Add Roasted Red Peppers and Chickpeas:
- Spoon the roasted red peppers and chickpeas onto each wrap.

Drizzle with Tahini Dressing:
- Drizzle a generous amount of the tahini dressing over the fillings.

Fold and Serve:
- Fold the sides of the wraps and roll them up tightly. Cut in half if desired and serve immediately.

Enjoy:
- Enjoy this delicious and nutritious Roasted Red Pepper and Chickpea Wrap!

This wrap is not only packed with vibrant flavors but also provides a good balance of protein, fiber, and wholesome ingredients. Customize it with your favorite veggies and enjoy a tasty and satisfying meal.

Turkey and Spinach Meatballs

Ingredients:

For the Meatballs:

- 1 pound ground turkey (preferably lean)
- 1 cup fresh spinach, finely chopped
- 1/2 cup breadcrumbs (whole wheat or gluten-free)
- 1/4 cup grated Parmesan cheese
- 1/4 cup finely chopped onion
- 2 cloves garlic, minced
- 1 large egg
- 1 teaspoon dried oregano
- 1 teaspoon dried basil
- Salt and black pepper to taste
- Olive oil for cooking

For the Sauce (optional):

- 1 can (14 oz) crushed tomatoes
- 1 clove garlic, minced
- 1 teaspoon dried Italian herbs (oregano, basil, thyme)
- Salt and black pepper to taste

Instructions:

For the Meatballs:

    Preheat Oven:
- Preheat your oven to 400°F (200°C).

    Prepare Ingredients:
- In a large mixing bowl, combine ground turkey, chopped spinach, breadcrumbs, Parmesan cheese, chopped onion, minced garlic, egg, dried oregano, dried basil, salt, and black pepper. Mix well until all ingredients are evenly combined.

    Shape Meatballs:
- Using your hands, shape the mixture into meatballs, about 1 to 1.5 inches in diameter. Place them on a baking sheet lined with parchment paper.

    Bake:
- Bake the meatballs in the preheated oven for 20-25 minutes or until they are cooked through and golden brown.

    For a Golden Crust (Optional):

- If you prefer a golden crust, you can sear the meatballs in a skillet with a bit of olive oil for 2-3 minutes on each side after baking.

For the Sauce (Optional):

Prepare Sauce:
- In a saucepan, combine crushed tomatoes, minced garlic, dried Italian herbs, salt, and black pepper. Simmer the sauce over low heat for about 10-15 minutes.

Add Meatballs to Sauce:
- Once the meatballs are baked, add them to the sauce and let them simmer for an additional 5 minutes.

Serving:

Serve:
- Serve the Turkey and Spinach Meatballs on their own or over your favorite pasta, rice, or salad.

Garnish:
- Garnish with additional grated Parmesan cheese and fresh herbs if desired.

Enjoy:
- Enjoy these delicious and healthier Turkey and Spinach Meatballs!

These turkey and spinach meatballs are a versatile option that pairs well with various dishes. Whether served with a classic tomato sauce, on a bed of pasta, or as a protein-packed salad topping, they make for a tasty and nutritious meal.

Sweet Potato and Black Bean Quesadillas

Ingredients:

- 2 medium-sized sweet potatoes, peeled and diced
- 1 can (15 oz) black beans, drained and rinsed
- 1 red onion, finely chopped
- 1 bell pepper (any color), diced
- 2 cloves garlic, minced
- 1 teaspoon ground cumin
- 1 teaspoon chili powder
- Salt and black pepper to taste
- 4 large whole wheat or corn tortillas
- 1.5 cups shredded cheese (cheddar, Monterey Jack, or a Mexican blend)
- Olive oil for cooking
- Optional toppings: Avocado slices, salsa, sour cream, cilantro

Instructions:

Roast Sweet Potatoes:
- Preheat your oven to 400°F (200°C). Toss the diced sweet potatoes with olive oil, salt, and pepper. Spread them on a baking sheet in a single layer. Roast for about 20-25 minutes or until the sweet potatoes are tender and slightly caramelized.

Prepare Filling:
- In a skillet over medium heat, sauté the chopped red onion and bell pepper in olive oil until softened, about 3-4 minutes. Add minced garlic, ground cumin, and chili powder. Stir in the black beans and roasted sweet potatoes. Cook for an additional 2-3 minutes until well combined. Season with salt and black pepper to taste.

Assemble Quesadillas:
- Heat a large skillet or griddle over medium heat. Place a tortilla on the hot surface. Sprinkle a layer of shredded cheese on one half of the tortilla. Spoon the sweet potato and black bean mixture over the cheese. Add another layer of cheese on top. Fold the tortilla in half, creating a quesadilla.

Cook Quesadillas:
- Cook each quesadilla for 2-3 minutes on each side or until the tortilla is crispy, and the cheese is melted.

Repeat:

- Repeat the process for the remaining tortillas and filling.

Slice and Serve:
- Once cooked, slice the quesadillas into wedges. Serve hot with optional toppings such as avocado slices, salsa, sour cream, and fresh cilantro.

Enjoy:
- Enjoy these delicious Sweet Potato and Black Bean Quesadillas as a flavorful and nutritious meal!

These quesadillas are not only a great vegetarian option but also a fantastic way to incorporate sweet potatoes and black beans into your diet. The combination of flavors and textures makes for a satisfying and wholesome meal.

Grilled Vegetable Platter with Hummus

Ingredients:

For the Grilled Vegetables:

- 1 zucchini, sliced
- 1 yellow squash, sliced
- 1 red bell pepper, sliced
- 1 yellow bell pepper, sliced
- 1 red onion, sliced into rings
- Cherry tomatoes
- 2 tablespoons olive oil
- 1 teaspoon dried oregano
- 1 teaspoon dried thyme
- Salt and black pepper to taste

For the Hummus:

- 1 can (15 oz) chickpeas, drained and rinsed
- 2 tablespoons tahini
- 2 tablespoons olive oil
- 2 cloves garlic, minced
- Juice of 1 lemon
- Salt and black pepper to taste
- Water (to adjust consistency)

Optional Garnishes:

- Fresh parsley, chopped
- Kalamata olives
- Feta cheese, crumbled

Instructions:

For the Grilled Vegetables:

Preheat Grill:
- Preheat your grill to medium-high heat.

Prepare Vegetables:

- In a large bowl, toss the sliced zucchini, yellow squash, red bell pepper, yellow bell pepper, red onion, and cherry tomatoes with olive oil, dried oregano, dried thyme, salt, and black pepper.

Grill Vegetables:
- Place the vegetables on the preheated grill. Grill for about 5-7 minutes, turning occasionally, until the vegetables are tender and have grill marks.

Remove from Grill:
- Remove the grilled vegetables from the grill and arrange them on a serving platter.

For the Hummus:

Prepare Hummus:
- In a food processor, combine chickpeas, tahini, olive oil, minced garlic, lemon juice, salt, and black pepper. Blend until smooth. If the hummus is too thick, you can add water, one tablespoon at a time, until you reach your desired consistency.

Adjust Seasoning:
- Taste the hummus and adjust the seasoning if needed, adding more salt, pepper, or lemon juice to suit your taste.

Assembling the Platter:

Serve Hummus:
- Spoon the freshly prepared hummus onto the center of the grilled vegetable platter.

Garnish (Optional):
- Garnish the hummus with chopped fresh parsley, Kalamata olives, and crumbled feta cheese.

Serve:
- Serve the Grilled Vegetable Platter with Hummus immediately. You can enjoy the vegetables and hummus with pita bread, crusty bread, or as a side dish.

Enjoy:
- Enjoy this colorful and flavorful Grilled Vegetable Platter with creamy hummus!

This dish is perfect for entertaining, as it's not only delicious but also visually appealing. The combination of smoky grilled vegetables and creamy hummus creates a satisfying and wholesome meal.

Shrimp and Avocado Salad

Ingredients:

For the Shrimp:

- 1 pound large shrimp, peeled and deveined
- 1 tablespoon olive oil
- 2 cloves garlic, minced
- 1 teaspoon smoked paprika
- Salt and black pepper to taste
- Lemon wedges (for serving)

For the Salad:

- 2 avocados, diced
- 1 cup cherry tomatoes, halved
- 1 cucumber, diced
- 1/4 cup red onion, finely chopped
- Fresh cilantro or parsley, chopped (for garnish)

For the Dressing:

- 3 tablespoons olive oil
- 2 tablespoons fresh lemon juice
- 1 tablespoon red wine vinegar
- 1 teaspoon Dijon mustard
- 1 clove garlic, minced
- Salt and black pepper to taste

Instructions:

For the Shrimp:

Marinate Shrimp:
- In a bowl, toss the peeled and deveined shrimp with olive oil, minced garlic, smoked paprika, salt, and black pepper. Let it marinate for about 15-20 minutes.

Cook Shrimp:

- Heat a skillet or grill pan over medium-high heat. Cook the shrimp for 2-3 minutes per side or until they are opaque and cooked through. Remove from heat.

Serve Shrimp:
- Squeeze fresh lemon juice over the cooked shrimp and set aside.

For the Salad:

Prepare Vegetables:
- In a large bowl, combine diced avocados, cherry tomatoes, diced cucumber, and finely chopped red onion.

Add Shrimp:
- Add the cooked shrimp to the bowl with the vegetables.

For the Dressing:

Prepare Dressing:
- In a small bowl, whisk together olive oil, fresh lemon juice, red wine vinegar, Dijon mustard, minced garlic, salt, and black pepper.

Dress Salad:
- Pour the dressing over the shrimp and vegetable mixture. Gently toss everything together until well coated.

Serving:

Garnish and Serve:
- Garnish the Shrimp and Avocado Salad with chopped fresh cilantro or parsley.

Serve:
- Serve the salad immediately, either on its own or over a bed of mixed greens.

Enjoy:
- Enjoy this light and flavorful Shrimp and Avocado Salad!

This salad is perfect for a quick and healthy meal, and it's a great option for lunch or dinner. The combination of shrimp, avocado, and fresh vegetables creates a satisfying and vibrant dish.

Spaghetti Squash with Tomato and Basil Sauce

Ingredients:

For the Spaghetti Squash:

- 1 medium-sized spaghetti squash
- Olive oil
- Salt and black pepper to taste

For the Tomato and Basil Sauce:

- 2 tablespoons olive oil
- 3 cloves garlic, minced
- 1 can (28 oz) crushed tomatoes
- 1 teaspoon dried oregano
- 1 teaspoon dried basil
- 1/2 teaspoon red pepper flakes (optional, for some heat)
- Salt and black pepper to taste
- Fresh basil, chopped (for garnish)
- Grated Parmesan cheese (optional, for serving)

Instructions:

For the Spaghetti Squash:

Preheat Oven:
- Preheat your oven to 400°F (200°C).

Prepare Spaghetti Squash:
- Cut the spaghetti squash in half lengthwise. Scoop out the seeds with a spoon.

Season and Roast:
- Drizzle the cut sides of the spaghetti squash with olive oil and sprinkle with salt and black pepper. Place the squash halves, cut side down, on a baking sheet. Roast in the preheated oven for 35-45 minutes or until the squash is tender and easily pierced with a fork.

Scrape and Fluff:
- Once cooked, use a fork to scrape the flesh of the spaghetti squash into "spaghetti" strands. Fluff and separate the strands.

For the Tomato and Basil Sauce:

Sauté Garlic:
- In a saucepan, heat olive oil over medium heat. Add minced garlic and sauté for about 1 minute until fragrant.

Add Crushed Tomatoes:
- Pour in the crushed tomatoes. Stir in dried oregano, dried basil, red pepper flakes (if using), salt, and black pepper.

Simmer:
- Bring the sauce to a simmer, then reduce the heat to low. Let it simmer for 15-20 minutes, allowing the flavors to meld and the sauce to thicken.

Adjust Seasoning:
- Taste the sauce and adjust the seasoning as needed.

Serving:

Combine and Garnish:
- Pour the tomato and basil sauce over the fluffed spaghetti squash. Toss gently to coat the squash with the sauce.

Garnish:
- Garnish with chopped fresh basil and, if desired, grated Parmesan cheese.

Serve:
- Serve the Spaghetti Squash with Tomato and Basil Sauce immediately.

Enjoy:
- Enjoy this light and healthy alternative to traditional pasta!

This dish is not only delicious but also a great option for those looking to reduce their carbohydrate intake or incorporate more vegetables into their meals. The tomato and basil sauce adds a burst of flavor, making the spaghetti squash a satisfying and wholesome choice.

Lentil and Kale Stuffed Bell Peppers

Ingredients:

For the Stuffed Bell Peppers:

- 4 large bell peppers, halved and seeds removed
- 1 cup green or brown lentils, cooked
- 2 cups kale, finely chopped
- 1 onion, finely chopped
- 2 cloves garlic, minced
- 1 can (14 oz) diced tomatoes, drained
- 1 teaspoon ground cumin
- 1 teaspoon smoked paprika
- Salt and black pepper to taste
- Olive oil for cooking

For the Sauce:

- 1 can (14 oz) tomato sauce
- 1 teaspoon dried oregano
- 1 teaspoon dried basil
- Salt and black pepper to taste

Optional Toppings:

- Grated cheese (cheddar or mozzarella)
- Fresh parsley, chopped

Instructions:

For the Stuffed Bell Peppers:

Preheat Oven:
- Preheat your oven to 375°F (190°C).

Prepare Bell Peppers:
- Cut the bell peppers in half lengthwise, removing the seeds and membranes. Place them in a baking dish.

Sauté Onion and Garlic:
- In a skillet, heat olive oil over medium heat. Add chopped onion and minced garlic. Sauté until the onion is translucent.

Cook Lentils and Kale:

- Add cooked lentils, chopped kale, diced tomatoes, ground cumin, smoked paprika, salt, and black pepper to the skillet. Cook for 5-7 minutes until the kale is wilted and the mixture is well combined.

Stuff Bell Peppers:
- Spoon the lentil and kale mixture into each bell pepper half, pressing down gently.

For the Sauce:

Prepare Sauce:
- In a bowl, mix together tomato sauce, dried oregano, dried basil, salt, and black pepper.

Pour Sauce:
- Pour the tomato sauce mixture over the stuffed bell peppers, ensuring they are well coated.

Bake:
- Cover the baking dish with foil and bake in the preheated oven for 30-35 minutes or until the bell peppers are tender.

Optional Toppings:
- If desired, sprinkle grated cheese over the stuffed bell peppers during the last 10 minutes of baking. Garnish with fresh parsley before serving.

Serving:

Serve:
- Serve the Lentil and Kale Stuffed Bell Peppers hot.

Enjoy:
- Enjoy this wholesome and plant-based meal!

These stuffed bell peppers are rich in protein from the lentils and packed with vitamins and minerals from the kale. The combination of flavors and textures makes for a satisfying and nutritious dish.

Chicken and Quinoa Lettuce Wraps

Ingredients:

For the Chicken and Quinoa Filling:

- 1 cup quinoa, rinsed and cooked according to package instructions
- 1 pound ground chicken
- 1 tablespoon olive oil
- 1 onion, finely chopped
- 2 cloves garlic, minced
- 1 red bell pepper, diced
- 1 carrot, grated
- 1 zucchini, diced
- 1 teaspoon ground cumin
- 1 teaspoon chili powder
- Salt and black pepper to taste
- 2 tablespoons soy sauce or tamari
- 1 tablespoon hoisin sauce
- 2 green onions, sliced
- Fresh cilantro, chopped (optional)

For the Lettuce Wraps:

- Large lettuce leaves (such as iceberg or butter lettuce)
- Sriracha sauce (optional, for serving)
- Lime wedges (for serving)

Instructions:

For the Chicken and Quinoa Filling:

Cook Quinoa:
- Rinse quinoa and cook according to package instructions. Set aside.

Sauté Chicken:
- In a large skillet, heat olive oil over medium heat. Add ground chicken and cook until browned, breaking it apart with a spoon.

Add Aromatics:
- Add chopped onion and minced garlic to the skillet. Sauté for a few minutes until the onion is translucent.

Add Vegetables:

- Add diced red bell pepper, grated carrot, and diced zucchini to the skillet. Cook until the vegetables are tender.

Season:
- Season the mixture with ground cumin, chili powder, salt, and black pepper.

Combine Quinoa:
- Stir in the cooked quinoa, soy sauce (or tamari), and hoisin sauce. Mix well and let it cook for a few more minutes.

Finish with Fresh Ingredients:
- Add sliced green onions and chopped cilantro (if using). Stir to combine.

For the Lettuce Wraps:

Assemble:
- Spoon the chicken and quinoa filling into large lettuce leaves.

Serve:
- Serve the lettuce wraps with Sriracha sauce on the side for those who enjoy extra heat. Garnish with lime wedges.

Enjoy:
- Enjoy these Chicken and Quinoa Lettuce Wraps as a flavorful and healthy meal!

These lettuce wraps are not only delicious but also customizable based on your preferences. Packed with protein from the chicken and quinoa, and loaded with colorful vegetables, they make for a satisfying and wholesome dish.

Roasted Beet and Goat Cheese Salad

Ingredients:

For the Salad:

- 4 medium-sized beets, peeled and diced
- 2 tablespoons olive oil
- Salt and black pepper to taste
- 8 cups mixed salad greens (such as arugula, spinach, or mixed greens)
- 1/2 cup candied pecans or walnuts, chopped
- 1/4 cup red onion, thinly sliced
- 4 ounces goat cheese, crumbled

For the Dressing:

- 3 tablespoons balsamic vinegar
- 1 tablespoon Dijon mustard
- 1 clove garlic, minced
- 1/2 cup extra-virgin olive oil
- Salt and black pepper to taste

Instructions:

For the Roasted Beets:

Preheat Oven:
- Preheat your oven to 400°F (200°C).

Prepare Beets:
- Peel and dice the beets into bite-sized pieces.

Toss with Olive Oil:
- In a bowl, toss the diced beets with olive oil, salt, and black pepper.

Roast:
- Spread the beets in a single layer on a baking sheet. Roast in the preheated oven for 25-30 minutes or until the beets are tender and caramelized, stirring halfway through.

Cool:
- Allow the roasted beets to cool to room temperature.

For the Dressing:

Prepare Dressing:

- In a small bowl, whisk together balsamic vinegar, Dijon mustard, minced garlic, salt, and black pepper.

Add Olive Oil:
- While whisking, slowly drizzle in the extra-virgin olive oil to emulsify the dressing.

Assembling the Salad:

Prepare Greens:
- In a large salad bowl, toss the mixed salad greens with half of the prepared dressing.

Arrange Components:
- Arrange the cooled roasted beets, candied pecans or walnuts, red onion slices, and crumbled goat cheese over the dressed greens.

Drizzle Dressing:
- Drizzle the remaining dressing over the assembled salad.

Toss Gently:
- Gently toss the salad to combine all the ingredients evenly.

Serve:
- Serve the Roasted Beet and Goat Cheese Salad immediately.

Enjoy:
- Enjoy this vibrant and flavorful salad as a refreshing and nutritious meal!

This salad not only offers a beautiful presentation but also a harmonious blend of sweet, tangy, and savory flavors. The roasted beets provide a rich, earthy taste, complemented by the creamy goat cheese and the crunch of candied pecans or walnuts. It's a perfect salad for a light lunch or as a side dish for a dinner party.

Miso-Glazed Eggplant

Ingredients:

- 2 medium-sized eggplants, sliced into rounds or wedges
- 2 tablespoons white or red miso paste
- 2 tablespoons mirin (Japanese sweet rice wine)
- 1 tablespoon soy sauce
- 1 tablespoon rice vinegar
- 1 tablespoon maple syrup or honey
- 1 tablespoon sesame oil
- 2 cloves garlic, minced
- 1 tablespoon ginger, grated
- Sesame seeds and chopped green onions for garnish
- Cooking oil (vegetable or sesame oil) for brushing the eggplant

Instructions:

Preheat Oven:
- Preheat your oven to 400°F (200°C).

Prepare Eggplant:
- Slice the eggplants into rounds or wedges, depending on your preference. Place them on a baking sheet lined with parchment paper.

Brush with Oil:
- Lightly brush the eggplant slices with cooking oil to prevent sticking and enhance the roasting process.

Roast Eggplant:
- Roast the eggplant in the preheated oven for about 20-25 minutes or until they are tender and golden brown.

Prepare Miso Glaze:
- While the eggplant is roasting, prepare the miso glaze. In a bowl, whisk together miso paste, mirin, soy sauce, rice vinegar, maple syrup or honey, sesame oil, minced garlic, and grated ginger.

Glaze Eggplant:
- Once the eggplant is done roasting, brush the miso glaze generously over each slice. Make sure to coat both sides.

Broil (Optional):
- If you desire a caramelized finish, you can broil the glazed eggplant for an additional 2-3 minutes until the top is slightly charred.

Garnish:

- Sprinkle sesame seeds and chopped green onions over the glazed eggplant for added flavor and presentation.

Serve:
- Serve the Miso-Glazed Eggplant warm as a side dish or over a bed of rice.

Enjoy:
- Enjoy the delicious combination of umami-rich miso and tender, caramelized eggplant!

This Miso-Glazed Eggplant recipe offers a unique and flavorful twist to this versatile vegetable. The sweet and savory glaze complements the mild bitterness of the eggplant, creating a dish that's both satisfying and packed with umami goodness.

Cabbage and Apple Slaw

Ingredients:

For the Slaw:

- 1/2 head green cabbage, thinly sliced or shredded
- 1 large apple, julienned or grated
- 1 carrot, julienned or grated
- 1/2 red onion, thinly sliced
- 1/4 cup fresh parsley, chopped (optional)

For the Dressing:

- 1/3 cup mayonnaise
- 2 tablespoons apple cider vinegar
- 1 tablespoon Dijon mustard
- 1 tablespoon honey or maple syrup
- Salt and black pepper to taste

Optional Add-ins:

- 1/2 cup raisins or dried cranberries
- 1/4 cup chopped walnuts or pecans

Instructions:

Prepare Vegetables and Apple:
- Thinly slice or shred the green cabbage, julienne or grate the apple, julienne or grate the carrot, and thinly slice the red onion. If using parsley, chop it finely.

Combine Ingredients:
- In a large bowl, combine the sliced cabbage, julienned apple, julienned carrot, sliced red onion, and chopped parsley.

Prepare Dressing:
- In a small bowl, whisk together mayonnaise, apple cider vinegar, Dijon mustard, honey or maple syrup, salt, and black pepper. Adjust the sweetness and acidity according to your taste.

Toss with Dressing:
- Pour the dressing over the cabbage, apple, and carrot mixture. Toss everything together until well coated with the dressing.

Optional Add-ins:

- If desired, add raisins or dried cranberries for sweetness and chopped nuts (walnuts or pecans) for extra crunch. Toss again to incorporate.

Chill:
- Allow the slaw to chill in the refrigerator for at least 30 minutes to allow the flavors to meld.

Serve:
- Serve the Cabbage and Apple Slaw chilled.

Enjoy:
- Enjoy this crisp and flavorful slaw as a side dish or a topping for sandwiches, tacos, or grilled meats.

Cabbage and Apple Slaw is a versatile dish that adds a burst of freshness to your meals. The combination of crunchy cabbage, sweet apples, and a tangy dressing makes it a perfect accompaniment to a variety of dishes, and it's particularly great for picnics or barbecues.

Baked Teriyaki Salmon

Ingredients:

For the Teriyaki Sauce:

- 1/4 cup soy sauce
- 3 tablespoons mirin (Japanese sweet rice wine)
- 2 tablespoons sake or dry white wine
- 2 tablespoons brown sugar
- 1 tablespoon honey
- 1 teaspoon grated ginger
- 1 teaspoon minced garlic
- 1 teaspoon cornstarch (optional, for thickening)

For the Salmon:

- 4 salmon fillets
- Salt and black pepper to taste
- Sesame seeds and chopped green onions for garnish (optional)

Instructions:

For the Teriyaki Sauce:

  Combine Ingredients:
  - In a small saucepan, whisk together soy sauce, mirin, sake or white wine, brown sugar, honey, grated ginger, and minced garlic.

  Simmer:
  - Bring the mixture to a simmer over medium heat. Allow it to simmer for 3-5 minutes until the sauce thickens slightly.

  Optional Thickening:
  - If you prefer a thicker sauce, you can dissolve cornstarch in a tablespoon of water and add it to the sauce. Stir well and simmer for an additional 1-2 minutes until thickened. Remove from heat.

For the Salmon:

  Preheat Oven:
  - Preheat your oven to 400°F (200°C).

  Prepare Salmon Fillets:

- Pat the salmon fillets dry with a paper towel. Season them with salt and black pepper.

Place in Baking Dish:
- Place the seasoned salmon fillets in a baking dish lined with parchment paper or lightly greased.

Brush with Teriyaki Sauce:
- Brush the teriyaki sauce generously over each salmon fillet, coating them well.

Bake:
- Bake in the preheated oven for 12-15 minutes or until the salmon is cooked through and flakes easily with a fork.

Broil (Optional):
- If you desire a caramelized finish, you can broil the salmon for an additional 2-3 minutes until the top is slightly charred.

Garnish:
- Garnish with sesame seeds and chopped green onions if desired.

Serve:
- Serve the Baked Teriyaki Salmon over rice or alongside your favorite vegetables.

Enjoy:
- Enjoy this delicious and glazed teriyaki salmon for a quick and satisfying meal!

Baked Teriyaki Salmon is a versatile dish that pairs well with various sides, and it's perfect for a quick and flavorful weeknight dinner. The homemade teriyaki sauce adds a delightful sweetness and umami to the salmon, making it a family-friendly favorite.

Broccoli and Cauliflower Gratin

Ingredients:

- 1 head of broccoli, cut into florets
- 1 head of cauliflower, cut into florets
- 2 tablespoons butter
- 2 tablespoons all-purpose flour
- 2 cups milk (whole or 2% recommended)
- 1 cup shredded sharp cheddar cheese
- 1/2 cup grated Parmesan cheese
- 1 teaspoon Dijon mustard
- Salt and black pepper to taste
- 1/4 teaspoon nutmeg (optional, for added flavor)
- 1 cup breadcrumbs
- Chopped fresh parsley for garnish (optional)

Instructions:

Preheat Oven:
- Preheat your oven to 375°F (190°C).

Steam Vegetables:
- Steam the broccoli and cauliflower florets until they are just tender. This can be done by blanching in boiling water or using a steamer. Drain and set aside.

Make Cheese Sauce:
- In a saucepan, melt the butter over medium heat. Add the flour and whisk continuously to form a roux. Cook the roux for 1-2 minutes, but do not let it brown.

Add Milk:
- Gradually whisk in the milk to the roux, ensuring there are no lumps. Continue whisking until the mixture thickens.

Add Cheeses and Seasoning:
- Reduce the heat to low. Add the shredded cheddar cheese, grated Parmesan cheese, Dijon mustard, salt, black pepper, and nutmeg (if using). Stir until the cheeses are melted and the sauce is smooth.

Combine Sauce and Vegetables:
- In a large mixing bowl, combine the steamed broccoli and cauliflower with the cheese sauce. Gently fold until the vegetables are coated evenly.

Transfer to Baking Dish:

- Transfer the mixture to a greased baking dish, spreading it out evenly.

Prepare Topping:
- In a small bowl, mix the breadcrumbs with a bit of melted butter. Sprinkle the breadcrumb mixture evenly over the top of the vegetable and cheese mixture.

Bake:
- Bake in the preheated oven for 20-25 minutes or until the top is golden brown, and the gratin is bubbly.

Garnish and Serve:
- Garnish with chopped fresh parsley if desired. Serve the Broccoli and Cauliflower Gratin hot.

Enjoy:
- Enjoy this comforting and cheesy gratin as a delicious side dish!

This Broccoli and Cauliflower Gratin is a crowd-pleaser and makes a perfect accompaniment to roasted meats or as a standalone vegetarian dish. The combination of creamy cheese sauce, tender vegetables, and crispy breadcrumb topping creates a delightful texture and flavor contrast.

Quinoa and Black Bean Burgers

Ingredients:

For the Quinoa and Black Bean Patties:

- 1 cup quinoa, cooked and cooled
- 1 can (15 oz) black beans, drained and rinsed
- 1/2 cup breadcrumbs
- 1/4 cup red onion, finely chopped
- 1/4 cup bell pepper (any color), finely chopped
- 2 cloves garlic, minced
- 1 teaspoon ground cumin
- 1 teaspoon chili powder
- 1/2 teaspoon paprika
- Salt and black pepper to taste
- 1 egg (or a flaxseed egg for a vegan option)
- 2 tablespoons olive oil (for cooking)

For Serving:

- Burger buns
- Lettuce, tomato slices, onion, avocado, or any preferred toppings
- Condiments (ketchup, mustard, mayo, etc.)

Instructions:

Prepare Quinoa:
- Cook quinoa according to package instructions. Allow it to cool to room temperature.

Mash Black Beans:
- In a large bowl, mash the black beans with a fork or potato masher until mostly smooth but with some texture remaining.

Combine Ingredients:
- Add the cooked quinoa, breadcrumbs, chopped red onion, chopped bell pepper, minced garlic, ground cumin, chili powder, paprika, salt, black pepper, and the egg (or flaxseed egg) to the mashed black beans. Mix well until all ingredients are combined.

Form Patties:

- Divide the mixture into equal portions and shape them into burger patties. Ensure that the patties hold together well. If the mixture is too wet, you can add more breadcrumbs.

Chill Patties (Optional):
- For a firmer texture, you can chill the patties in the refrigerator for at least 30 minutes.

Cook Patties:
- In a skillet, heat olive oil over medium heat. Cook the quinoa and black bean patties for 4-5 minutes on each side or until they are golden brown and cooked through.

Assemble Burgers:
- Toast the burger buns and assemble your burgers with the quinoa and black bean patties. Add your favorite toppings and condiments.

Serve:
- Serve the Quinoa and Black Bean Burgers hot.

Enjoy:
- Enjoy these delicious and nutritious veggie burgers!

These Quinoa and Black Bean Burgers are not only packed with protein and fiber but also full of flavor. Customize your burgers with your preferred toppings and condiments for a satisfying and wholesome meal.

Grilled Turkey and Veggie Kabobs

Ingredients:

For the Turkey Marinade:

- 1 pound turkey breast, cut into cubes
- 3 tablespoons olive oil
- 2 tablespoons soy sauce
- 2 tablespoons honey
- 2 cloves garlic, minced
- 1 teaspoon dried thyme
- 1 teaspoon smoked paprika
- Salt and black pepper to taste

For the Veggie Kabobs:

- Cherry tomatoes
- Bell peppers, cut into chunks (use various colors)
- Red onion, cut into chunks
- Zucchini, sliced into rounds
- Mushrooms, cleaned and halved
- Olive oil for brushing
- Salt and black pepper to taste

Other:

- Wooden or metal skewers (if using wooden skewers, soak them in water for 30 minutes before grilling)

Instructions:

For the Turkey Marinade:

    Prepare Marinade:
- In a bowl, whisk together olive oil, soy sauce, honey, minced garlic, dried thyme, smoked paprika, salt, and black pepper.

    Marinate Turkey:
- Place the turkey cubes in a shallow dish or a resealable plastic bag. Pour the marinade over the turkey, ensuring it is well-coated. Marinate in the refrigerator for at least 30 minutes, or ideally, 2-4 hours.

For the Veggie Kabobs:

- Prepare Veggies:
  - While the turkey is marinating, prepare the vegetables by cutting them into uniform-sized pieces.
- Assemble Kabobs:
  - Thread the marinated turkey cubes and the prepared vegetables onto the skewers, alternating between turkey and veggies.
- Brush with Olive Oil:
  - Brush the assembled kabobs with olive oil and season with salt and black pepper.

Grilling:

- Preheat Grill:
  - Preheat your grill to medium-high heat.
- Grill Kabobs:
  - Grill the turkey and veggie kabobs for about 10-15 minutes, turning occasionally, until the turkey is cooked through and the vegetables are tender and slightly charred.
- Serve:
  - Remove the kabobs from the grill and let them rest for a few minutes. Serve them hot.
- Enjoy:
  - Enjoy these flavorful and juicy Grilled Turkey and Veggie Kabobs as a delightful and healthy meal!

Feel free to customize the vegetables based on your preferences, and you can serve these kabobs with a side of rice, quinoa, or a refreshing salad for a complete meal.

Zesty Cilantro Lime Cauliflower Rice

Ingredients:

- 1 medium-sized head of cauliflower, riced (or you can use pre-riced cauliflower)
- 2 tablespoons olive oil
- 3 cloves garlic, minced
- 1/2 cup red onion, finely chopped
- Juice of 2 limes
- Zest of 1 lime
- 1/4 cup fresh cilantro, chopped
- Salt and black pepper to taste

Instructions:

Prepare Cauliflower Rice:
- If you haven't already, rice the cauliflower by using a food processor or a box grater. Alternatively, you can use pre-riced cauliflower.

Sauté Aromatics:
- In a large skillet or pan, heat olive oil over medium heat. Add minced garlic and chopped red onion. Sauté for 2-3 minutes until the onion is translucent.

Cook Cauliflower Rice:
- Add the riced cauliflower to the skillet. Cook for 5-7 minutes, stirring occasionally, until the cauliflower is tender but not mushy.

Zest and Lime Juice:
- Zest one lime directly into the cauliflower rice. Then, cut the zested lime in half and squeeze the juice over the rice. Stir well to combine.

Add Cilantro:
- Stir in the chopped cilantro, distributing it evenly throughout the cauliflower rice.

Season:
- Season the cauliflower rice with salt and black pepper to taste. Adjust the seasoning according to your preference.

Serve:
- Transfer the Zesty Cilantro Lime Cauliflower Rice to a serving dish.

Garnish (Optional):
- Garnish with additional cilantro and lime wedges if desired.

Enjoy:

- Serve as a side dish alongside your favorite protein or use it as a base for bowls, burritos, or tacos.

This Zesty Cilantro Lime Cauliflower Rice is not only a tasty alternative to traditional rice, but it also adds a burst of freshness and flavor to your meals. It's a versatile dish that pairs well with various cuisines and can be customized based on your preferences.

www.ingramcontent.com/pod-product-compliance
Lightning Source LLC
LaVergne TN
LVHW081604060526
838201LV00054B/2070